Framing and Interpretation

Interpretations

This series provides clearly written and up-to-date introductions to recent theories and critical practices in the humanities and social sciences.

General Editor
Ken Ruthven (University of Melbourne)

Advisory Board
Tony Bennett (Griffith University)
Penny Boumelha (University of Adelaide)
John Frow (University of Queensland)
Sneja Gunew (University of Victoria, British Columbia)
Robert Hodge (University of Western Sydney)
Terry Threadgold (Monash University)

Already published:
Cultural Materialism, by Andrew Milner
Metafictions?, by Wenche Ommundsen
Nuclear Criticism, by Ken Ruthven
A Foucault Primer, by Alec McHoul and Wendy Grace
After Mabo, by Tim Rowse
Masculinities and Identities, by David Buchbinder

In preparation:
Multicultural literature studies, by Sneja Gunew
Postmodern socialism, by Peter Beilharz
Discourses of science and literature, by Damien Broderick
The body in the text, by Anne Cranny-Francis
Post-colonial literature, by Anne Brewster
Feminist film theory, by Barbara Creed

Framing and Interpretation

Gale MacLachlan
and Ian Reid

MELBOURNE UNIVERSITY PRESS
1994

First published 1994
Designed by text-art
Typeset by text-art in 10½ point Garamond
Printed in Malaysia by SRM Production Services Sdn Bhd for
Melbourne University Press, Carlton, Victoria 3053
U.S.A. and Canada: International Specialized Book Services Inc.,
5804 N.E. Hassalo Street, Portland, Oregon 97213-3644
United Kingdom and Europe: University College London Press,
Gower Street, London WC1E 6BT

ISSN 1039-6128

National Library of Australia Cataloguing-in-Publication data

MacLachlan, Gale L. (Gale Lorraine), 1944– .
    Framing and interpretation.
    Bibliography.
    Includes index.
    ISBN 0 522 84576 2.
    1. Discourse analysis. 2. Criticism. 3. Semiotics. I. Reid,
    Ian, 1943– . II. Title. (Series: Interpretations.).
808.0014

For Nola Bartlett
and Iris O'Shea

Contents

Acknowledgements .... *xi*

1 'Framing Occurs, but there is no Frame' *1*

Where interpretation meets framing *1*
Material and metaphorical frames *5*
A new view of 'context' *6*
The semiotic framework *10*
Interpreting 'interpretation' *11*
Maintaining the frame *12*
A deconstructive paradox *15*
Framing the frame *17*

2 Framing Visual Signs *19*

Frames and painting *19*
The frame as focusing device *20*
Frames and genre *21*
The value-added gilt frame *22*
The semiotic function of frames *23*
The 'intra-compositional' frame *24*
Who controls the frame? *25*
Frames and the 'logic of supplementarity' *26*
Framing the viewer *27*
Breaking the frame *28*
Intertextual frames *29*

Contents

The art gallery as frame 31
Other circumtextual frames 32
Movietime: the temporal viewing frame 34
The dry quadrilateral 36
Soundtracks and other framing elements 37

3 Framing Experience: 'What is it that's
Going on Here?' 40
Two theoretical affiliations 40
Frames as metamessages: Gregory Bateson 41
Reframing experience 45
Frame analysis: Erving Goffman 46
Combat or play? A question of keying 48
Out-of-frame activity 51
Frame-breaking 52
Insider's folly 53
The frame paradox revisited 54
Frames as 'brackets' 55
Errors of framing 56
Context revisited 58
Framing Goffman 59
Framing conversation: Deborah Tannen 60
Your frame or mine? 63
Metamessages and meta-metamessages 64
Framing and reframing: a dynamic process 65
What's in a frame? 65

4 Knowledge Frames and Framing Knowledge 68
A new collaborative field 68
Top-down and bottom-up processing 69
Frames for representing knowledge 71
Frame semantics or checklist theories? 73
Cognitive frames and framing 75
Framing educational knowledge: Basil Bernstein ... 77
Power at the margins 79
Disciplinary frames 80
Reframing texts in the classroom 83

Contents

5 Generic Framings of Written Texts 85

Insurance against risk 85
The case of epitaphs 86
The case of poetry 90
The case of literary prose 92
Borderline deceptions 94
Frames within frames 97
Intertextual framings 101
Paratextuality and postmodernist prose 103

6 Markers, Metamessages and Mediation 106

Texts are always mediated 106
The politics of cultural mediation 109
'Frames are always framed': the issue of authority 111
Mediated and 'unmediated' communication 112
Tourism and the quest for unmediated experience 113

Bibliography 116
Index 126

Acknowledgements

We are indebted to Ken Ruthven as series editor for his thorough and encouraging attention to our manuscript; to Wenche Ommundsen for helpful comments on an early draft portion; to Venetia Nelson for her careful checking of the final typescript; and to Wendy Waring for reliable research assistance at several stages of the work.

Our thanks go also to the institutions that gave us support in various ways during the writing of this book: Macquarie University, Curtin University of Technology, and the University of Western Australia. Over a longer period, colleagues and students at these places have provided a congenial environment for developing the ideas that find expression in the following pages.

Acknowledgements

1

'Framing Occurs, but there is no Frame'

Where interpretation meets framing

Most of us are seldom conscious of the extent to which even the simplest communication depends on complex interpretive processes. These processes, it will be argued, depend in turn on various kinds of framing. Consider the following mini-story:

(1) *Duval went into the restaurant. He ordered pasta and a glass of red wine. He asked the waitress for the bill and left.*

At first sight, narrative sequences such as this would seem to pose no problems of comprehension whatever. And yet the ability to process such a sequence and make immediate sense of it presupposes more than purely linguistic knowledge about the meanings of the individual words and the syntactical connections between them. On closer inspection it is obvious that nowhere in the actual sentences that make up this narrative can we find all the information needed to understand it. If we were to feed this story into a computer which had been programmed only with the grammar of the relevant language, there would be significant gaps in its comprehension of the events described. For what would be missing in such a computer program is the real-world knowledge of restaurant-going behaviour (among other things), against which the actions in our story must be framed for the appropriate inferences to be drawn.

Such real-world knowledge, built up on the basis of experience of similar occasions, makes it possible to infer the events elided from the story sequence. Given their familiarity with what generally happens in restaurants, readers automatically supply these missing links, which are assumed by the text in the interests of narrative economy. It is therefore unnecessary for the story to specify that Duval presumably waited to be seated, consulted the menu, ordered a meal from a waitress, was served, ate his meal and paid for it before leaving. Other intermediate steps and variants on this sequence could be adduced by individual readers.

Researchers in the area of cognitive science, investigating the ways in which everyday knowledge of this kind is stored and organised in the human memory, posit the existence of what have been variously called 'frames', 'scripts', 'schemata' and so on (Minsky, 1980; Schank and Abelson, 1977; Bartlett, 1932; Tannen, 1979). Terminology may vary, but cognitive scientists generally agree that knowledge of stereotypical situations like restaurant-going, rather than being scattered as separate items of information throughout the memory, is organised in directly accessible units (Brown and Yule, 1983:236). The 'restaurant script' is an example of the kind of knowledge unit accessed by a reader in understanding a simple story like the above. There are many other so-called 'cognitive frames' for storing and organising everyday knowledge which readers automatically draw upon in any act of interpretation. Frames exist for such things as birthday parties, supermarket shopping, movie-going and countless other ordinary activities. (Chapter 4 will discuss some limitations of cognitive frame theory.)

But this is only part of the story. Understanding even very simple texts involves much more than the activation of background knowledge of this kind. More fundamental perhaps is the generic frame we call up when we assign story (1) to a particular type, the 'theoretical example'; that is, when we regard it as a text used to illustrate a particular point in a certain kind of expository prose. Framing it in this way automatically imposes constraints on the way we interpret what we read; the same sequence encountered as, say, the opening sentence of a detective novel would command a very different kind of attention, generating meanings one would not expect to be activated by its presence in a book such as this.

Consider another short sequence of a very different type:

(2) *(Husband): I had an interesting lunch at Peppers today . . .*
    (Wife): Blonde or brunette?

To interpret this elliptical exchange, much more is involved than the simple activation of a restaurant frame which the words 'lunch at Peppers' might initially call to mind. (Indeed it would be hard to imagine being able to program a computer in such a way that it could make any sense of this sequence at all.) The inferences a reader has to make here relate to scripts or frames of a different kind, since understanding the exchange between this couple involves, among other things, imputing to the wife an act of interpretation about the nature of the husband's lunch which would make sense of her seemingly *non sequitur* reply. In other words, the married status of the two speakers will lead the reader to infer that story (2) concerns a couple whose intimate knowledge of each other permits an interpretive act which would most likely be inappropriate in other circumstances. One might presume that the wife is framing her husband's statement against her knowledge of his past behaviour, which leads her to assume that the presence of a woman is the source of his 'interesting' lunch. 'Blonde or brunette?' then is not so much a question as a statement which not only asserts the wife's ability to interpret a seemingly innocent comment but may also suggest cynical detachment, playful teasing, or even a relationship of knowing complicity with him. One could speculate further about this exchange, but its status as a 'theoretical example' in a book of the present kind puts limits on the process of interpretation.

   In the case of written and spoken texts, therefore, interpretation is clearly more than just an application of the linguistic knowledge necessary to decode words and to make connections between them and the sentences in which they are embedded. As we will argue throughout this book, acts of *extratextual framing* are always involved—'extratextual' in the sense that they depend on seemingly 'outside' (*extra*) information, unspecified by the text but felt to be presupposed by it: the term is explained more fully in the next chapter. Whatever we read, we frame extratextually by drawing on our accumulated knowledge of the world, both experiential and textually mediated. This activity may include, among other things, matching a particular sequence of events to some stereotypical script as well as provisionally assigning it to a particular text-type or genre.

Another kind of framing, which by contrast can be called *intratextual*, occurs when we pay attention to the way in which the flow of words 'within' (*intra*) the text is affected by subdivisional or other internal framing devices. This, too, will need more precise discussion as our analysis proceeds. There is a simple example in story (2): both utterances are framed by the parenthetical specifications 'husband' and 'wife', which guide our interpretation of the dialogue. It can of course act as a cue only if we simultaneously bring extratextual knowledge of stereotypical husband–wife behaviour to our reading of the text. Both kinds of framing are necessary.

But that is not all. If we happen to recognise story (1) as a variation on the routine 'restaurant example' much exploited in the theorisings of cognitive scientists like Schank and Abelson, we are framing it *intertextually* (*inter*, 'between'). Intertextual frames relate one text or text-type to another. In this instance, intertextual framing not only establishes the generic status of that particular mini-story but also links the book you are now reading with a certain kind of theoretical discourse. Again, it is only through extratextual knowledge of this discursive field that an intertextual connection can be established here.

In addition, our reading of a text can be framed for us by the *circumtextual* features (*circum*, 'around') of its material presentation and location in space. For example, the title of this book and the presence of references, a bibliography and an index, as well as the kind of bookshop where it is sold, all contribute to the way readers interpret the information it contains. These framing cues help to establish the scholarly affiliations of the book, distinguishing it from, say, popular fiction.

Interpretation of the simplest utterances depends therefore on acts of framing of which readers are generally unaware, and which are often beyond their control. In Chapter 5, which focuses on the framing of written texts, we will attempt to refine and develop the four kinds of framing we have proposed above, with particular emphasis on the complex ways in which they interact with each other in any act of interpretation.

Material and metaphorical frames

We have focused so far on relatively simple metaphorical uses of the term 'frame' as a way of understanding what is involved in the interpretation of oral and written texts. Let us consider next some more intricate examples of framing which concern the work of a painter, indicating their complexities without pausing at this stage to explicate them all. Combined in this set of examples are some aspects of material or literal *frames* involved in the presentation of non-verbal texts like paintings and photographs, and also some remarks on how these actual frames can indicate the more complex *framings* that may occur in a viewer's mind.

We begin with a photograph that brings together images of two famous avant-garde artists from different times and places. Taken in a museum devoted to one of these artists, the nineteenth-century French poet Arthur Rimbaud, it shows the Australian painter Brett Whiteley standing naked except for a framed portrait of Rimbaud held in front of his face. Reproduced in books and articles on Whiteley, this simple visual joke can be interpreted as a comment on some of the ways in which any interpretation itself depends on framing.

Whiteley's gesture, viewed through the technical framing device of a camera lens, appears to indicate playfully that he wishes to place his own artistic career and creative work within a particular context—of avant-garde aesthetic practice, of personal notoriety as a bohemian *enfant terrible*— for which Rimbaud is a recognisable emblem. This frame of reference, asking us to interpret the twentieth-century Australian painter by associating him with the earlier French writer, becomes more pertinent when we know that one of Whiteley's paintings refers directly to Rimbaud, incorporating a portrait of him and making the link explicit in its title. Whiteley has also put in writing some admiring comments on Rimbaud; and these, too, provide a certain frame through which to view the modern artist and his productions.

Of course any act of framing may be reframed in turn to suggest a different interpretation. Alluding unmistakably to the photograph just discussed, and to Whiteley's apparent cultivation of celebrity status in the Sydney artworld, the newspaper cartoonist Arthur

Horner once depicted him holding an empty picture frame around his head and shoulders, above this satirical clerihew as a caption:

> Brett Whiteley
> gives performances nightly
> in the art of living out one's fame
> in a frame.

Yet more is involved in this set of interpretive framings. For example, the gesture of affiliation—enacted by Whiteley in that Rimbaud museum, recorded by the photographer and reproduced in a book—has a reciprocal effect as well. While Whiteley invokes the sign 'Rimbaud' as a frame for his own activity as a painter, there is also a converse sense in which Rimbaud is being posthumously framed by Whiteley's attentions. This illustrates a principle of reframing stated by T. S. Eliot: that the past is 'altered by the present as much as the present is directed by the past' (1953:24). Or, to use a similar formulation by the Argentinian writer Jorge Luis Borges: 'every writer *creates* his own precursors' (1970:236).

Such variations on the theme of Whiteley's links with Rimbaud demonstrate the general point that frames may take several material or non-material forms, of which the viewer may sometimes be only subliminally aware. Each gives its particular shape to the meanings of whatever object, space or situation it encloses. As the French philosopher Jacques Derrida has aphoristically stated: 'Il y a du cadre mais le cadre n'existe pas' (1978:83)—which can be translated as 'Framing occurs, but there is no frame'. There is no frame, first because framing is an *act* rather than a stable given, and second because even solid, material frames tend to be naturalised by the viewer into near oblivion. As we will see in later chapters, this quasi-invisibility is true of all frames, both metaphorical and material.

A new view of 'context'

Cognitive scientists tell us that theories about 'knowledge-structures' such as frames, and their role in understanding, stem from 'a recognition that context is of overwhelming importance in the interpretation of text' (Schank and Abelson, 1977:9). A similar emphasis on 'context' may seem to characterise those contemporary literary theorists who reject the notion of the text as a stable, self-sufficient entity and shift attention instead to how texts are framed by the more pragmatic circumstances of their production and reception. And yet, while it may be true that for cognitive scientists the notion of 'context' continues to be unproblematically invoked, for contemporary literary theorists it has undergone a complete rethinking in accordance with the view 'that our relationship to reality is not a positive knowledge but a hermeneutic construct, that all perception is already an act of interpretation' (Freund, 1987:5).

Jonathan Culler is one such critic who draws attention to the 'heuristically simplifying presumptions' of the term 'context' in the preface to his book *Framing the Sign: Criticism and its Institutions*. It is worth quoting at length the reasons for his dissatisfaction with this term as an explanatory principle:

> The opposition between an act and its context seems to presume that the context is given and determines the meaning of the act. We know, of course, that things are not so simple: context is not fundamentally different from what it contextualizes; *context is not given but produced*; what belongs to a context is determined by interpretive strategies; contexts are just as much in need of elucidation as events; and the meaning of a context is determined by events. Yet when we use the term 'context' we slip back into the simple model it proposes. (Culler, 1988:ix, italics added)

If context is 'not fundamentally different from what it contextualizes', being no more stable or determinate than the text with which it is connected or brought into connection, then text/context distinctions begin to break down. There is a sense therefore in which any context is simply more 'text', constituted as it is by an act of selection which presupposes interpretation. This is presumably the point of Derrida's cryptic maxim *il n'y a pas de hors-texte* —literally, 'there is no outside of the text'.

What Culler proposes in place of 'context' is the more active term 'framing', which emphasises agency and process. 'Framing the sign', part of the title of his book, is a way of describing the interpretive process which, he suggests, has the advantage of emphasising what we *do* with texts (and, we might add, what texts *do* with us). In other words, what such a term draws attention to is the *priority* of acts of framing, since such acts determine what we perceive to be the context(s) for any cultural object or event. When teachers of literature used to talk about giving students 'the' context before tackling a text of a particular period, perhaps remote in time and place to their own, they were implying that the context of its production was a single, clearly locatable and stable field, innocent of any act of interpretation. Given the 'textual' nature of the field (and this is the sense of Derrida's remark), acts of interpretation are shaped, among other things, by the ideology of the interpreter, who carries around as part of his or her extratextual baggage what Norman Fairclough calls 'a mental map of the social order'. 'Such a mental map', he writes, 'is necessarily just one interpretation of social realities which are amenable to many interpretations, politically and ideologically invested in particular ways' (Fairclough, 1992:83).

The contexts of the text's reception are also variable, given all the situational factors at work affecting interpretation: socio-cultural circumstances, institutional settings, the class, gender and race of the interpreter and so on. Another variable is the way in which, as we have seen in the Whiteley example, the context for a given text (whether verbal or visual) is always being modified by its ongoing relationships with other similar texts. A precursor text, like a Rimbaud poem, frames the Whiteley painting and photograph; conversely the photograph alters our perception of the precursor's significance. Such relationships may or may not be signalled explicitly. Yet another aspect of intertextuality is that the context for reading a text changes continually as new critical readings accumulate. Further, texts may attempt to situate themselves—to control our interpretation of them by 'producing', through various framing devices, contexts appropriate to their reading (Chambers, 1984:207).

In summary: a text does not have a single meaning determined by a single context; given the interplay of different framings, contexts and therefore meanings are multiple. Thus the term 'context' is often unsatisfactory, not only because it is too broad and imprecise to be of much use in clarifying what is at issue in interpreting texts, but also because its static connotations tend to obscure the dialectical nature of the text–context relationship. For just as a text is shaped and constrained by the various contexts of its production and reception, so also does each text contribute to the very constitution of the contexts which shape and constrain it (Fairclough, 1992:ch. 3). Moreover, while we may frame the reading of texts in particular ways, this activity is not independent of the devices by which texts may attempt to frame themselves. Emphasis on 'framing', rather than on 'context', draws attention to agency and acknowledges the complex nature of the interpretive process. There is always a dynamic interaction (potentially a struggle to shape meaning) between text and interpreter, text and context.

The fact that written texts frame themselves in various ways in an attempt to control our interpretation of them is a result of their being alienated from the original circumstances of their production. Unlike face-to-face communication, where a speaker's (conscious) intentions or meanings may be checked against the utterance, written texts are cut off from their original situation, 'orphaned, and separated at birth from the assistance of the father', to use Derrida's paternal metaphor (1982:316). This orphaned status, however, is precisely what creates the conditions that enable interpretation to occur. But it is also what makes interpretation potentially uncontrollable, and so texts attempt to regulate the proliferation of meanings in ways that we will examine more fully later.

Culler concludes that a further advantage of the term 'framing' is that it alludes to the semiotic function of framing in art, 'where the frame is determining, setting off the object or event as art, and yet the frame itself may be nothing tangible, pure articulation' (Culler, 1988:iv). This is reminiscent of Derrida's formulation that framing occurs, but there is no frame. Some of the framings associated with the Whiteley example above demonstrate the 'intangibility' Culler refers to here. In Chapter 2 we will examine the art gallery/museum as an example of a more tangible 'framing' location within which objects—even quite ordinary, everyday artefacts—acquire the status of 'art'.

It may seem disappointing that Culler's book, despite the promise of its title, never properly theorises the substitute term 'framing', which tends to drop out of his analyses altogether as the book progresses. However, as his own introduction candidly acknowledges, there are real difficulties with a project of 'framing the sign', for 'analysis can seldom live up to the complexities of framing and falls back into discussion of context' (ibid.:ix).

The semiotic framework

We should not let Culler's remarks deter us from attempting to sort out some of the complexities of a term that has been invoked by theorists in almost every area of the humanities and the social sciences over the last couple of decades. Such widespread interest in the metaphor of framing reflects the recent shift away from considering texts as finished 'products' towards an emphasis on the 'processes' of their production and interpretation. ('Text' is now generally taken to include not only any instance of oral and written discourse but also any other cultural practice or artefact.) Common to all these disciplines is the desire to investigate not so much *what* things mean, but *how* they come to mean in the first place, and the connections between the two.

How meanings are produced and recognised in society is the subject of that science of signs which is called *semiotics*. It marks a fundamental shift away from the positivist principle that meaning is inherent in a phenomenon, waiting there to be extracted by the attentive interpreter, towards the semiotic principle that a phenomenon acquires its capacity to signify x or y only by being placed within a system of conventional relationships among signs. These sign systems are the cultural codes which make it possible for an object or event to be meaningful. In the case of verbal texts, as we have seen with the 'restaurant' narratives quoted at the beginning of this chapter, language is only one of the signifying systems through which texts acquire meaning. Generic codes are another. So too are the broader social codes which regulate eating, fashion, sex, sport and so on.

A man raises his hand: what does this gesture mean? The question cannot be answered unless we obtain further information, which would need to indicate *how* (that is, within which sign system, including particular social or cultural settings) the meaning is being generated. If the person who raises his hand is evidently taking a pre-eminent role within a certain public ritual, we could say that the action means 'a regal wave to a crowd of commoners'; if the person is engaged in a formal business meeting, the significance of the raised hand may be 'a vote in favour of a motion'; if he is an actor playing a villain's part in some drama, we will construe the gesture as 'threat of violence to another person'; if he is playing basketball, he may be asking a team-mate for the ball, or pretending to ask a team-mate for the ball so as to distract an opponent, or trying to intercept an opponent's pass . . .

Each of these meanings (the 'what') depends on our recognition or adducing of a signifying framework, a gestural code (the 'how') relevant to the particular situation and culture. This enables us to recognise the raised hand as meaningful rather than to ignore it as a random gesture which is semiotically neutral. Problems arise of course when we misframe gestures according to cultural codes that are inappropriate to the situation, or when we have doubts about the semiotic status of an action in a particular context. In a classroom setting, for instance, the raised hand may indicate that the student is merely stretching (which is not necessarily a semiotically neutral gesture since it may signify boredom) or is wanting to ask a question or be excused.

Simple gestures may signify differently in other cultures: sitting with one's foot pointing towards another person in the room may be semiotically neutral in one culture but semiotically loaded in another. Part of the foreign language teacher's task—and the function of diplomatic briefings—is to acquaint students and others with the repertoire of gestures that carry significance in the culture concerned.

What the signifying frameworks are, *who* controls them and *how* they are activated by the reader or viewer are the sorts of issues relevant to frame theorists. As we will see, different theoretical perspectives determine which of these questions receives primary emphasis in a particular disciplinary area. Issues concerning the politics of framing, the power relations involved in the struggle for control of meaning, will be addressed in the final chapter.

Interpreting 'interpretation'

So fundamental to the humanities and social sciences is the activity of interpretation that it has itself been continually interpreted over a long period by philosophers, historians, linguists, literary critics, and indeed by theorists of every disciplinary and interdisciplinary persuasion. The present book, being merely a survey, does not claim to offer any comprehensive analysis of that range of theories. Our specific concern here is with the meeting-point between interpretation and framing.

There is a critical tradition, no longer dominant, which treats interpretation as a 'hermeneutic' enterprise—that is, as a process of understanding and explaining texts on the assumption that meaning is inherent in them and needs to be brought to light by interpretive procedures. This emphasis on revealing hidden sig–nificance is usually linked by hermeneuticists with the principle that the 'intention' of the text's producer is what a 'valid' interpretation must discover. Hermeneutic approaches, which go back through the nineteenth-century German philosophers Friedrich Schleiermacher and Wilhelm Dilthey to medieval practitioners of biblical exegesis, are represented in more recent times by the work of critics such as Hans-Georg Gadamer (1975), Paul Ricoeur (1974), Richard Palmer (1969) and E. D. Hirsch (1967). Its general decline coincides with the rapid rise of semiotics, which regards meaning as constructed by an interpreter on the basis of textual and other signs. In the course of a clear discussion of this important shift in contemporary theory and critical practice, David Bordwell sums up the matter neatly: the prevailing view now is that 'meanings are not found but made' (1989:3). It is within this perspective that terms such as 'frame' have become particularly attractive.

Maintaining the frame

Using metaphors of framing to elucidate what happens in the interpretive process suggests, as noted earlier, an analogy with the material borders that shape and surround works of art. Framing a painting can be seen as an act of enclosure that serves to demarcate a semiotic field, separating it from the rest of the plane against which it is viewed and thereby telling us how to regard it. As Gregory Bateson puts it, we can consider the frame around a picture 'as a message intended to order or organize the perception of the viewer', a message which 'says, "Attend to what is within and do not attend to what is outside." . . . Perception of the ground must be positively inhibited and perception of the figure (in this case the picture) must be positively enhanced' (Bateson, 1972:187).

With similar emphasis, John Frow remarks that a frame 'can be anything that acts as a sign of qualitative difference, a sign of the boundary between a marked and an unmarked space'. In the case of literary texts, fictional space is thus set off from reality by the use of various framing devices like titles, subtitles and prefaces and specific locations in libraries and bookshops; the aesthetic space of a painting is bordered by the frame, setting it off from the extra-aesthetic space of the wall, which in turn may be part of a room within a gallery; sculptures are often placed on plinths in special places inside and outside galleries or churches, and so on. Frow concludes that 'any aesthetic object or process will tend to be defined by a particular configuration of framings' (1986:220).

Many common socio-cultural practices could be similarly defined. Take, for example, the gynaecological examination. Such occasions clearly involve 'a particular configuration of framings' so that the exposing of one's sexual organs to what might be a perfect stranger is clearly understood by all parties to be a medical rather than an erotic encounter. Constraints such as the setting in which such examinations take place (usually in a room separate from the room in which the doctor and patient meet and discuss any problems), who is permitted to take part in the examination, the topics which can be discussed, the kind of language used and other non-verbal gestures are all part of a standardised set of procedures to ensure that misinterpretation does not occur. Norman Fairclough in *Language and Power* (1989) discusses such examinations in detail, pointing out that 'medical staff show their disengagement in the quality of their *gaze*, the professionally appraisive (rather than aesthetically evaluative) way in which they look at the patient's body'. Just as medical staff handle the patient's body in brisk and efficient ways, so too must the patient observe similar protocols. Breaking the highly conventionalised frame of these encounters by, for instance, making eye contact at the 'wrong' moment or exhibiting or touching the body in the 'wrong' space is likely to effect a change in the meaning of that encounter (Fairclough, 1989:59).

Many other examples of similarly defined semiotic fields, unrelated to aesthetic experience, are to be found in everyday life. Analyses of them differ in emphasis according to disciplinary orientation. From the perspective of a discourse analyst like Fairclough, the conventions defining genres or 'discourse types' like the medical examination or the job interview are associated with social institutions, which in turn are shaped ideologically by power relations. A sociologist like Erving Goffman is more interested in the way an individual's framing of events establishes their meaning for him or her. Goffman analyses 'the special vulnerabilities to which these frames of reference are subject' (1974:10). By 'special vulnerabilities' he means, among other things, misframings (intentional as well as the simply erroneous), frame 'traps' (confidence tricks and the like) and frame-breaking of various kinds. Some of these will be surveyed in Chapter 3, but at this stage an example of frame-breaking and its significance in the field of sport, analysed in detail by Goffman, may help to clarify what is at stake in the maintenance or violation of cultural frames.

Exhibition wrestling matches exemplify the systematic violation of the traditional boundaries that constitute the semiotic field of 'serious' game time/space. Conventionally these spatio-temporal frames were maintained in wrestling as in boxing, with fighting occurring only between the ceremonial beginning and end of the match, and within the spatial boundaries established by the ropes and elevated stage on which the opponents meet. Audience interaction was also restricted by the same spatio-temporal bracketing. In exhibition wrestling, however, these boundaries seem only to be maintained enough 'to give meaning to violations, and violations abound' (ibid.:417). Even the umpire (in 'serious' sports a mostly 'out of frame' director of the proceedings) has his directives not only continuously ignored, but is himself the subject of attack by the wrestlers in 'a monstrous infraction of framing rules' (ibid.):

> Traditionally when one wrestler was pushed off the mat, a tap on the shoulder of the advantaged man given by the referee would break the game, and the men would reassemble in proper array well within the mat boundary (the disadvantaged man on all fours and the other free to take a hold). Should a wrestler happen

to fall out of the ring—a rare occurrence—the contestants would immediately go out of frame, and the courtesies of the street, not the ring, would come into force . . . In exhibition wrestling . . . wrestlers routinely step or crawl outside the ropes to force a stopping of the match. They are routinely thrown out of the ring into the audience or escape imminent doom by the same route. Once outside the ropes (and even the ring) they take up afresh their quarrel with the audience, the umpire, and the opponent, the last sometimes joining the ousted enemy in order to continue the fight. (ibid.:418)

Such a display, together with the ongoing theatrical differentiation of the two wrestlers into 'heavy and hero', is not a display of wrestling skill at all, but entertainment of a different kind which comes from subverting 'sometimes magnificently and sometimes cathartically' the traditional frame of serious wrestling. It is interesting to note that Roland Barthes (1972), in a famous analysis of wrestling as a spectacle of excess, invokes a quite different interpretive frame from Goffman's. For Barthes, exhibition wrestling is the 'true' wrestling, to be distinguished from serious or 'false wrestling' as well as from boxing.

Traditional frames of a different kind are similarly subverted when fiction-writers indulge in direct audience address, violating the diegetic (story) boundaries observed by more conventional writers. The popularity of such tactics is confirmed by the phenomenal sales of detective story parodists like San-Antonio in France who, in the guise of author/narrator, harangues and harasses the reader in a variety of entertaining ways (see MacLachlan, 1993). One of the interesting aspects of frame-breaking practices, as these last two examples demonstrate, is the way in which regular subversions of traditional genres may be instrumental in the generation of popular new ones.

A deconstructive paradox

The general basis for regarding interpretive acts as acts of framing is therefore quite simple: when any cultural phenomenon, practice, or product (be it a written text, an art work, a medical interview or a sporting event) is made to mean something, this signifying process both separates it from and joins it with a variety of references. Metaphors of framing can aptly indicate that in order to perceive and understand anything we must provisionally distinguish it from other things while also relating it to them. Exhibition wrestling and literary parody produce their particular meanings by virtue of their difference from and similarity to more serious genres. Framing is thus the process of demarcating phenomena in a double-edged way that is simultaneously inclusive and exclusive.

In an essay called 'The Parergon', concerned with certain aesthetic questions posed by the philosopher Immanuel Kant, Derrida (1987) provides a useful perspective on the functions of frames in art and in perception, drawing particular attention to this 'double-edged' quality. The *parergon* (literally translatable as 'something alongside the work or *ergon*') is a concept briefly introduced by Kant, who uses it to refer to adjunctive ornamentation such as temple colonnades, clothes on statues, or picture frames. In Derrida's hands the concept is amplified and sophisticated, its paradoxical character emphasised, for the *parergon* is an element both extrinsic and intrinsic to a given object of attention, whether architectural, pictorial or anything else. This supplementary 'frame' is neither part of it nor apart from it, because it has no stable existence or location independent of the interpretive act which constitutes it. 'Its importance', says Frow in his commentary on Derrida's essay, 'lies precisely in this ambiguity of its threshold situation . . . The frame does not simply separate an outside from an inside but unsettles the distinction between the two' (Frow, 1986: 222–3). For example: think of any painting hung in a public space. Vis-à-vis the gallery wall, its border seems to belong to the interior of the artwork, but vis-à-vis the painted surface it seems part of the surroundings. In Chapters 2 and 5 we will discuss some of the border tensions that result from the inside-outside paradox in visual and verbal 'texts', noting the ways in which different frames interact with, and sometimes dissolve into, each other.

As his discussion of Derrida's *parergon* develops into a consideration of this concept 'as a metaphor for the frame structures of genre and the literary system' (ibid.:220), Frow stresses that the *parergon* is both 'a way of considering in "material" terms a set of abstract determinants and a way of formulating the paradox of systemic determination and of the textual modification of a system (so that the text is never the simple effect of its determinants, the inside of an outside)' (ibid.). That is to say, the paradoxical nature of the material frame helps us to understand how it is that texts are determined by their generic 'place' in the system of literary artefacts and yet, by their difference, modify the very system that helps to define them. For example, while detective stories must obey the requirement of same-yet-different that controls the production of formulaic fiction, each example of the genre modifies our perception of what to include under this rubric. Generic frames are therefore no more stable than contexts, since each results from a prior act of framing. We will take up this issue in Chapter 4 in our discussion of cognitive frames.

Framing the frame

In the last twenty years 'framing' metaphors have been a conceptual aid to many theorists concerned with issues of interpretation across the humanities and the social sciences. Unfortunately, however, the terms 'frame', 'framing' and 'framework' are often used imprecisely, and sometimes in highly specialised technical ways without much regard for other usages. Without entering at this stage into controversial areas of debate, we can nevertheless regard a 'frame', whether material or metaphorical, as the result of an act of 'framing', and a superordinate set of frames as a 'framework'. Our own preference is to use the term 'framing' wherever possible for reasons we have already suggested: 'framing' is an act which necessarily involves an agent and therefore implies something more provisional, more negotiable than the substantive term 'frame'.

Since the interdisciplinary implications of 'framing' metaphors are not fully explained in any accessible handbook, there is a need to sort out systematically the different senses involved and to provide a range of detailed illustrations from the various fields in which this terminology is current. The ensuing chapters aim therefore to summarise different applications of framing theory to cultural practices, with suggestions for further reading. We hardly need insist that no pretence is made of being able to treat such a large topic in an exhaustive way. But each chapter takes a major area in which framing concepts are applicable, and examines their relevance to a general theory of how interpretation occurs. Chapter 2 focuses on the frame as sign in the visual arts; Chapters 3 and 4 on framing in the social and cognitive sciences; chapter five on exemplary strategies for framing and reframing in the interpretation of literary and other written texts, and Chapter 6 on the inescapability of mediation and therefore of struggles for control of the frame.

We have also proposed, in a schematic way at the beginning of this chapter, our own model of the different framing operations involved in interpretation and how they interact with each other. This will be further developed in the chapters that follow, particularly in Chapter 5.

But first, let us consider the function of frames and framing in art.

2

Framing Visual Signs

Frames and painting

Think of a painting you have seen before in an art gallery, and ask yourself what kind of frame it had or whether indeed it had a frame at all. Probably you will have difficulty remembering. Why is this so? Why do frames, even when disproportionately large and ornately decorated, tend to become 'invisible'? Why are they seldom mentioned in catalogues or reproduced in art books? As a visit to an art gallery will reveal, a considerable effort of concentration is required in order to focus exclusively on frames, for what normally holds our attention is the figure rather than the ground (as Gestalt psychologists would put it)—that is, the framed object rather than the enclosing frame.

This quasi-invisibility of picture frames means that we tend to take their presence, form and effects for granted. We also take for granted the regular shape of the field they enclose. And yet, as Meyer Schapiro points out, 'such a field corresponds to nothing in nature or mental imagery where the phantoms of visual memory come up in a vague unbounded void' (1969:223). Historically speaking, the regular prepared field represents 'an advanced artefact presupposing a long development of art' (ibid.). The earliest examples of human art, the cave paintings of the Stone Age, were executed on a rough, unprepared surface with no definite boundaries. Cave artists, with their habit of painting over preexisting figures, showed little concern with the field as a distinct ground on which to paint their figures. Schapiro notes that the development of a smooth, bounded field accompanied the invention of tools in the Neolithic and Bronze Ages, the creation of pottery and an architecture that offered regular shapes and surfaces for decoration. Through the closure of a particular surface, the image came to occupy a delimited space of its own.

The frame and the regular margin were also relatively late inventions, appearing at the earliest in the latter part of the second millennium BC. The function of these material borders was to isolate and protect the image against encroachment from the surrounding space. At the same time, frames in their earliest forms were designed to harmonise with their architectural or decorative surroundings, providing a link or a transition space between the two. Heydenryk (1963) notes, in his richly illustrated history of frames, that wooden frames developed out of panel paintings in the thirteenth century, the raised rim of the hollowed-out surface serving to frame the image. It was soon realised however that 'applied frames', made out of separate pieces of wood, offered stronger support and better protection against cracking and warping. This led to the creation of the elaborately decorated altarpieces of the fourteenth and fifteenth centuries.

The frame as focusing device

As well as offering protection and support to the painted canvas, frames also have the power to affect our perception of what they enclose. There is, for example, a small landscape painting in the Art Gallery of Western Australia by Arthur Streeton entitled *From the Yarra across Melbourne Botanic Gardens*. This painting has a disproportionately large varnished frame whose colour, grainy texture and angled depth strongly resemble a window frame. A viewer who peers at the painting through such a frame has the illusion of glimpsing a real landscape through a real window.

When frames of this kind enclose pictures incorporating perspective, they help deepen the illusion of three-dimensionality. In this way they function as 'finding and focusing' devices belonging more to the space of the observing subject than to the world of the painting (Schapiro, 1969: 227). It is for this reason that, despite their prominence as material objects, they tend to be 'disattended' as the observer focuses on the represented scene. We might think of their near invisibility as similar to the way in which the proscenium arch, curtains and footlights in a theatre tend to be forgotten when we are watching a play. It would make little sense for frames of this perspectival type, since they affect the real-world viewing conditions of paintings, to be included in art books and catalogues.

Non-representational paintings, on the other hand, with their emphasis on the more formal or expressive aspects of line, colour and shape, have no need for the focusing device of the angled 'window' frame. Their minimal framing (or lack of a frame) emphasises their two-dimensionality and asserts their status as flat painted artefacts with little or no reference to the world outside their borders. As Schapiro states, 'if the painting once receded within the framed space, the canvas now stands out from the wall as an object in its own right' (ibid.). Not all non-representational art dispenses with the frame, however: some works have elaborate, recessed frames that reverse the traditional relationship between picture and frame. Some incorporate the wall as 'frame'. Others have narrow unobtrusive frames in the same plane as the canvas, whose simplicity, in Schapiro's view, 'asserts the respect for frankness and integrity in the practice of the art' (ibid.:228).

Frames and genre

Whatever the genre, symmetrical shape would seem to be the most persistent convention associated with the framing of paintings and photographs. Among the various shapes possible, it is the rectangle which predominates, for obvious practical reasons since it is easier to stretch a canvas over such a base. (In traditional landscape painting, the horizontal is half as long again as the vertical.) Oval, circular, semicircular, diamond, arched and octagonal shapes also occur in traditional painting, such departures from the rectangular 'norm' being most often associated with the portrait or, less commonly, the landscape. For this reason, when a contemporary painter like Pablo Picasso uses the oval shape (set in a rectangular frame) for a 'still life', a genre with which it is not normally associated, the formal relationship between rectangle and oval tends to be foregrounded—as, for example, in two guitar paintings executed in 1912. The viewer is inclined to interpret this unconventional choice as a means of focusing attention on the interplay between the curvaceous form of the 'body' of the musical instrument in tension with the taut horizontal lines of its strings and frets.

Asymmetrical frames and irregular surfaces are not very common in western art. When they do occur they can disturb the viewer, since they are reminders of conventions we generally naturalise to the point of amnesia. The Art Gallery of Western Australia holds a painting by Aboriginal artist Mavis Holmes Petyarre which uses as its framing surface a car door; this draws attention to the cultural specificity of any traditionally framed canvas, particularly as Petyarre's work is hung near several pictures with regular borders.

The value-added gilt frame

Not all elaborate frames fulfil the 'finding and focusing' function referred to above. There is, for example, in the Art Gallery of Western Australia a small dark painting of a nativity scene by the seventeenth-century painter Carlo Maratti which seems overwhelmed by an enormous black frame with flamboyant gilt leaves at each corner. Given its relative flatness and total lack of harmony with the scene depicted, such a frame appears to have no other function than to designate, through its gilded opulence, the painting's 'old master' status and hence to signal its cultural and economic worth.

Heavy, ornate gilt frames whose size and decoration often add nothing to the aesthetic enhancement of paintings can therefore be thought of as 'value-added' frames. So too are the 'finding and focusing' frames referred to above if similarly gilded and decorated. Such frames, used from the seventeenth century onwards, communicate 'metamessages'—messages about (*meta*) messages—that tell us how to evaluate or interpret what they enclose. (The term 'metamessage' will be taken up in more detail in Chapter 3.) There are of course other framing devices for indicating cultural and economic worth, such as the gallery or museum itself; but the elaborate gilt frame, for all that we tend to repress its presence, is the most conspicuous sign of a painting's prestige. Since such frames are mostly 'extra-compositional' (to use John Pearson's term) in the sense that they are added to the painting rather than a constitutive part of the actual composition, they locate control of the painting as aesthetic object and economic good in the proprietorial hands of the owner/consumer. This explains why, as Pearson points out, fairly inexpensive reproductions of masterpieces are often placed in large gilt frames:

> The frame as a sign of value enhances the worth of the copy by lending it meaning in the semiotics of economy . . . The frame's purpose . . . is to announce the closed tectonic border that is presumed to exist between the conceptual realm of art, which it contains, and the world, in which it suggests the function of art as commodity. (Pearson, 1990:17)

The semiotic function of frames

As Michael Carter remarks, it is a fundamental characteristic of visual imagery that 'unlike "reality" which appears as unbounded, the image constantly displays to its viewer the fact that it is different from "reality" by having an edge' (1990:149). The frame as a material reinforcement of this edge functions first and foremost as a device for distinguishing or setting off a certain kind of space—aesthetic space—from the surrounding area. Constituting a limit or boundary between the 'inside' and 'outside' of an art-form, it demarcates a perceptual field within which what is being looked at signifies differently. Frames are therefore constitutive of visual signs as well as having the potential to carry messages to the viewer about how these signs may be interpreted.

As we have seen, richly decorated gilt frames may assert that what they enclose is a culturally prestigious part of the art field and is within the proprietorial control of the consumer. But this is not the only possible message. Religious icons, for instance, are often enclosed by gold-leaf frames inset with precious stones which attest to the sacred nature of what is depicted. In the case of portraiture, gilt frames may be used to signal the wealth and power of the person portrayed, and/or the value of this individual to the owner of the portrait.

Frames can also be specific to the culture of origin, and those that are common in one culture may not be considered politically or aesthetically appropriate to the art works of another. If a gallery were to place an ornate gilt frame around an Australian Aboriginal painting, this would probably be taken to signify the appropriation of black culture by whites. The nineteenth-century New Zealand painter C. F. Goldie, though a *pakeha* himself, was conscious of such problems, and sought to avoid them by specifically designing special dark-stained frames for his portraits of Maoris. However, something different seemed necessary when he produced with L. J. Steele a huge canvas, *The Arrival of the Maoris in New Zealand*, a scene which unmistakably repeats the epic theme, compositional lines and figurative motifs of Géricault's famous *Raft of the Medusa*, painted eight decades earlier in France. This intertextual link is circumtextually reinforced by Goldie and Steele: their picture has a large gilt frame to testify to the 'classic' status of its style and subject.

Since no frame is semiotically neutral, the minimal or unobtrusive frame generally signifies modernity and is often associated, as we have seen, with non-representational genres. It may also suggest a kind of artistic integrity in its rejection of the aggrandising effect of the 'old master' frame. Even absent frames come to signify in various ways. 'Without a frame', Meyer Schapiro states, 'the painting appears more completely and modestly the artist's work' (1969:228). The absence of a frame can thus be a way for the artist to assert and to maintain control over the semiotic field of the painted canvas, a field over which (especially at the boundaries) there is inevitably a struggle for control.

The 'intra-compositional' frame

Another way of asserting control over the painting and its margins is for the artist to incorporate the whole field, borders and all, into the composition itself. The frame, while remaining separate from what is depicted, thus becomes inseparable from the composition as a whole. Unlike the adjunctive or 'extra-compositional' frames that belong to the world of the viewer/consumer, these 'intra-compositional' frames (Pearson, 1990:16) resist appropriation, remaining under the artistic control of the artist concerned.

There are many examples of such 'authorially' controlled frames; Celant (1982:54) discusses their salience in European art in the late nineteenth century. The Art Gallery of New South Wales holds a painting by Sir Edward Poynter entitled *The Visit of the Queen of*

Sheba to King Solomon (1890). This spectacular work (2.3 x 3.5 m) depicts the Queen inside a Greek-inspired classical temple mounting a flight of stairs flanked by golden lions to greet the King. The whole is enclosed by an extraordinarily extravagant Renaissance-inspired gilt frame that is 'architectural' in its effect since it incorporates classically decorated Greek pilasters and horizontals which repeat themes depicted in the painting. This picture is thus framed by a border whose flatness emphasises the fresco-like magnitude of the scene. At the same time, given its resemblance to the portals of a temple or classical theatre, it serves to enhance the dramatic effect of the famous encounter.

Poynter's specially designed frame is felt to be so integral to the composition itself that, in a departure from tradition, it is normally reproduced in art books and catalogues and specifically commented upon. (See, for instance, Renée Free's comments in the NSW Gallery's catalogue, *Victorian Olympians*.) A frame like this belongs not to the world of the viewer but rather to the world of the painting itself, with which it harmonises so perfectly that it too, despite (and because of) its unique form, tends nevertheless to be 'forgotten'.

Once again, it would seem that whether or not the frame of a painting is felt to be intrinsic or extrinsic to the work, in either case it is usually destined to near-invisibility, for reasons noted by Derrida in his discussion of the *parergon* (see p. 16).

Who controls the frame?

In the late nineteenth century, as Pearson has remarked, a number of painters of the 'representational' kind began to reappropriate the frame and/or the border areas of the canvas as a way of reasserting control over 'the art work as a semiotic field and an economic good' (1990:15). Such an annexing of formerly 'alien territory' by the artist can be explained, Pearson argues, as symptomatic of the historico-political context of the period which is characterised by the western imperialistic drawing of 'alien cultures and territories within the boundaries of national power' (ibid.:29). If Pearson's historical parallelism seems unconvincing, since the relationship between self and other is, in each case, fundamentally different, he nevertheless offers some interesting examples of artistic border tensions.

In the domain of painting, for instance, he points out that the realist painter Gustave Courbet attempted to produce more organically responsive frames to enclose his subjects. Freshly cut pine boughs frame one such composition. The early French Impressionists similarly rejected the tradition of the gilt frame, experimenting in different ways with incorporating the framing space into the composition itself. 'Neutral' white frames resembling the typographical margins of the printed page were used by Edgar Degas as a means of suppressing 'the proprietory discourse of the traditional frame by denying the border itself' (ibid.:19). Further, by using the technique of 'cropped' figures at the edges of the painting, Degas (like Toulouse-Lautrec and Renoir) draws attention to the borders of the frame, thereby giving prominence to *framing as an act* involving aesthetic choice, not just as a material border. For beyond the frame, it is suggested, extends an artistic continuum, the demarcation of which involves the authoritative exercise of a particular artistic consciousness. The 'modernity' of this consciousness stems from the fact that cropped scenes, strongly suggesting the fragmentary and the contingent, imply a different aesthetic, that of the momentary glance rather than the classic 'set' view or the more formally posed studio tableau (Schapiro, 1969:227).

Georges Seurat, on the other hand, not only reclaimed the frame as border but took over the margins as well for developing in an abstract pointilliste way a kind of 'painterly discourse that mediates between art and the world' (Pearson, 1990:19). While these painted margins are distinct from the representational discourse of the composition they enclose, they are nevertheless 'intra-compositional', being part of the composition though not part of the actual picture (ibid.:20). Like the mediating prefaces that accompany many literary texts of this period and earlier, Seurat's borders affirm the authority of his particular aesthetic vision and method.

Frames and the 'logic of supplementarity'

As Pearson points out, English Pre-Raphaelites such as William Morris and John Everett Millais resolved the problem of border tensions in a different way. Specially designed and individually handcrafted wooden frames, often decorated with motifs found in the painting itself, were produced as a kind of artistic supplement to the paintings they enclosed. Charles Collins, for instance, decorated the gold frame for his *Convent Thoughts* with lilies that repeat the motif of the pure white lilies in the painting itself. The inner rim of the frame forms an archway through which the nun may be seen pausing in her reading to examine a flower. (Intratextual frames such as doorways, windows, trellises and pictorial borders which draw attention to acts of artistic framing are also very common in the paintings of this school.)

The tendency throughout this period, Pearson observes (1990:22), is towards increasing control of the borderlines by integrating what was previously 'alien territory' into the composition itself. For an artist like Dante Gabriel Rossetti, this desire for control asserted itself not only through the construction of special frames but also through the inclusion of comments inscribed on the borders of paintings, designed to create the 'ideal viewer' of his work. Two sonnets, as well as symbolic motifs which are repeated in the canvas, adorn the frame for *The Girlhood of Mary Virgin*. Exploiting the resources of a different artistic medium, Rossetti explicates the symbolism of the painting in one sonnet, and expresses his intentions in the other. When marginalia constrain interpretation in this way, the frame becomes the site of an authoritative critical discourse. Through the principle that Derrida (1976:141) calls 'supplementarity', such discourse has the function of ensuring that the absent originator of the work survives in and around its margins.

Framing the viewer

There are, however, other ways of attempting artistic control over the way a painting or any other visual image is perceived. The organisation of elements within the pictorial field itself, both in relation to each other and to the viewing subject, determines how we see them. As Schapiro points out, 'the picture field has local properties that affect our sense of the signs. These are most obvious in the differences of expressive quality between broad and narrow, upper and lower, left and right, central and peripheral, the corners and the rest of the space' (1969:229). When we are faced with unbounded images such as cave drawings, we centre whatever image we happen to be looking at. When, on the other hand, we have a bounded field in view, the centre of that field is predetermined by the borders of the frame. The positioning of figures in relation to this centre affects our interpretation of and response to them. An off-centre figure, for instance, creates a sense of visual tension that may be interpreted, with the help of other cues, as expressing isolation, withdrawal, introversion. Schapiro cites the example of a painting by Edvard Munch, *Melancholy*, in which the figure of a man is seated off-centre, in profile, chin in hand. The rest of the picture offers an indeterminate landscape stretching away to the left of the figure with little to capture the eye. This pictorial void, in conjunction with the tension created by the decentred position of the figure, confirms the sense of spiritual emptiness and introversion suggested by the title. (Its 'intertextual' link with Albrecht Dürer's famous engraving *Melancholia* reinforces this sense.)

Some paintings exploit these spatial relationships to create unconventional viewing positions for the spectator. *Double Self Portrait*, for instance, by the contemporary Australian painter Howard Taylor, includes several peripheral frames as well as, most arresting of all, a rectangular frame around one of the eyes of the two overlapping profiles. The eye thus foregrounded seems to position the viewer uncomfortably as framed rather than as framing subject. In a similar way, Manet's *Olympia*, in returning the gaze of the viewer, breaks the convention of nude women as objects for the voyeuristic delectation of the public.

Other intratextual frames create unstable or impossible positions for the viewer. For example, John Brack's portrait *Red Carpet* is dominated, as the title suggests, by an obliquely angled red Persian carpet which backgrounds the distorted figure of a woman who is seated in an unsettling relationship to the viewer. There is no comfortable position from which to view the picture so as to make sense of it perceptually. In other words, the way in which this painting frames itself challenges the expectations we have of the figure–ground relationship in conventional portraits.

Breaking the frame

Frame-breaking is yet another way of asserting control over the borders of a visual image and of suggesting the problematic nature of simplistic inside/outside distinctions. (In Chapter 3 we take up this aspect of framing in more detail, with particular reference to Goffman's 1974 study.) When frame boundaries are transgressed, the frame tends to recede into the background as a pictorial element. Such a violation of conventional boundaries can function as an expressive device conveying a sense of dynamic movement when, for instance, a figure crosses the boundaries of pictorial space. As a result, 'the frame belongs . . . more to the virtual space of the image than to the material surface; the convention is naturalized as an element of the picture space rather than of the observer's space or the space of the vehicle' (Schapiro, 1969:228).

Such transgressions into frame space were apparently common in medieval as well as in classical art. In modern times, frame-breaking is not so easily 'naturalised'. The kind of frame-breaking practised by painters such as René Magritte, Max Ernst and others tends to suggest the instability of the border region itself as a threshold between frame and picture space. This is similar to the unstable visual field created in the drawings by the Dutch artist M. C. Escher, which causes the viewer to oscillate between conflicting figure–ground relationships within the frame of the drawings.

Intertextual frames

Paintings, like photographs and sculptures, also frame themselves 'intertextually'—that is to say, in relation to other works of art, media, or genres, often from a different era and/or cultural situation. In a sense, as we pointed out in Chapter 1, *all* texts, whether verbal or visual, rely on intertextual framing, being intelligible only by reference to prior texts or genres. But there are degrees of explicitness in this framing process: reference to a particular work will impose interpretive constraints of a different kind from simple generic affiliation.

One of the most common forms of intertextual framing encountered in painting is the direct homage paid to 'past masters' through imitation of well-known canvases. A recent exhibition at the Louvre entitled 'To Copy is to Create: From Turner to Picasso' displayed 300 works inspired by the great-master paintings held in the gallery. Certain famous works were regularly copied: Titian's *The Entombment*, for example, was reinterpreted by artists as various as Turner, Géricault, Cézanne, Derain and Chagall. In this exhibition, copies were hung alongside the originals (or photographic reproductions of them), their juxtaposition activating meanings that would other- wise have remained latent for the average gallery visitor viewing these paintings in isolation.

Intertextual framing may also occur more indirectly through allusive reference or quotation, sometimes in a different medium. Magritte, for instance, ironically 'quotes' David's celebrated portrait *Madame Récamier* by recasting elements of the original composi- tion in bronze and by substituting a coffin in the same pose as the recumbent lady. Another striking example of intertextual framing in a different medium, exhibited in the Art Gallery of Western Australia, is an extraordinarily lifelike sculpture by the noted North American realist John de Andrea, entitled *Allegory: after Courbet.* This work pays respectful tribute to one of the great realist paintings of the nineteenth century, Gustave Courbet's *The Painter's Studio: Allegory of Seven Years of my Artistic and Moral Life.* The original painting created a scandal in 1855 since it depicts the artist at work on a canvas in his studio watched by a child, a nude model and a crowd of fully dressed onlookers. As some of the impact of de Andrea's sculpture is lost if the viewer is unable to recognise the reference, there is an explanatory wall plaque with a photographic reproduction of the original close by. Like the didactically inclined Pre-Raphaelites, galleries also fulfil an educative function by attempting to produce the 'ideal viewer' of the works they offer for display.

One of the most literal examples of intertextual framing is Salvador Dali's 1926 painting *Couple with Heads full of Clouds.* Using two outlined figures from a well-known realist painting by Jean-François Millet, *The Angelus*, as frames containing typically Dali-esque dream landscapes, Dali suggests tension between the conventions of realism and the surreal world of fantasy and dream. *The Angelus* reappears in other Dali works, and so too does Jan Vermeer's famous painting *The Lacemaker*, whose needle he transforms into a rhinoceros's horn!

Probably the most quoted and most often (mis)appropriated painting of all is the *Mona Lisa*. Regarded in the twentieth century as a bourgeois icon of art, it has been subjected to all kinds of transgressive treatment. In 1919 Duchamp added a moustache, a wispy beard and a ribald inscription, and Fernand Léger reduced it to the status of an object by placing it in the same frame as a bunch of keys and a tin of sardines. From the 1950s onwards it appears in a number of American paintings, most notably in a work by Andy Warhol where an image of the original is multiplied to the point of utter banality.

The art gallery as frame

No matter how strictly individual artists may attempt to control the consumption of their work, they cannot succeed fully. Since painting, like literature, is cut off from the original circumstances of its production, it is vulnerable to reframing in the literal sense and, more metaphorically, to the reframing that occurs as a result of its placement in different semiotic 'fields'. The art gallery itself is one such field. How we view a painting is thus determined, as we have suggested above, by its presence in a particular space and its relation to other paintings and works of art in that space. When Turner donated many of his paintings to the National Gallery in London, he did so on the condition that they be displayed in close proximity to those of Claude Lorrain, whom he had imitated and emulated. More commonly though, paintings are hung together on the basis of historical or thematic groupings. These affiliations may be indicated by their placement in particular rooms in a gallery or by their inclusion in special collections or displays like the copyists exhibition referred to earlier.

The gallery can thus be thought of as a kind of circumtextual frame or semiotic space which, among other things, makes it possible to distinguish the *objet d'art* from similar or even identical everyday functional objects. Sometimes the difference between art object and its utilitarian counterpart is reinforced by an incongruous title or its unusual placement on a pedestal or overhead: some of Marcel Duchamp's *objets trouvés* or 'ready-mades' (bicycle wheels, urinals, etc.) are displayed in this way. Sometimes, like Andy Warhol's Brillo soap-pad boxes, they differ only in size. With certain sculptures or pop art installations, a white line on the floor surrounds the exhibit; in this way, aesthetic or 'hands-off' space is distinguished from the functional space of the gallery floor.

It is important to note that mundane or utilitarian objects on display need not differ in any way from their normal appearance in the world outside the gallery. What causes them to be perceived differently, as art objects, is the framing space of the gallery itself, together with any other adjunctive frames that set them apart from their 'real-world' counterparts. Similarly, in the case of collage art, it is the relocation of ephemera like newspaper clippings, tickets, bits of string or any other fragments of the world of our everyday experience inside an artistic frame that so fundamentally alters their status.

Other circumtextual frames

Sometimes, however, the simple presence of an object or group of objects in a gallery is not sufficient to confirm its artistic status. This is particularly so in the case of 'installation art', or in displaying artefacts commonly encountered in the world outside the art-space. If you see a ladder leaning on a gallery wall, how do you know whether it has been placed there for your aesthetic contemplation or for someone's mundane task?

In the Art Gallery of Western Australia there is a series of framed photographs of Los Angeles and New York, several of which are casually propped against the wall instead of being hung in the usual way. The inattentive visitor could be forgiven for assuming that these form part of a series of photographs in the process of being arranged for display. What constitutes them, however, as a 'finished' work is the presence of an identifying plaque on the wall nearby. This informs us that the artist responsible is Bill Henson, and that the sequencing of the individual items is meant to be variable, being left to the control of the gallery. We are also told that these 'unsettling representations of urban alienation' constitute a compo-sition which has been left untitled so as not to constrain the viewer's interpretation. Clearly the 'frame' that designates this collection of photographs as an art work is not only the gallery, but more importantly the accompanying written text. As this example shows, within the signifying space of the gallery itself written texts such as plaques, or the explanatory notes that frame different collections, have a double function: they both designate something as 'art' and guide our interpretation of it. Other kinds of 'circumtexts' which mediate our reception of a work include titles, signatures, cata-logues, museum guides and audiovisual commentaries.

Titles are especially important in controlling the interpretation of what we see. Sometimes tensions are created by unexpected relationships between a title and the visual composition itself. There is a painting by John Byam Shaw in the Pre-Raphaelite tradition which depicts with photographic clarity a woman standing pensively by the banks of a stream bordered by the cool green and mauve luxuriance of bush and blossom. It bears the seemingly incongruous title *The Boer War* and, like so many paintings of this school, was further framed by a poetic text—some lines from Christina Rossetti—when it was exhibited in 1901:

> Last summer green things were greener
> Brambles fewer, the blue sky bluer.

The interaction of the title and verse caption leads the viewer to interpret the painting not just as a kind of elegy for the war dead in the war to which the title refers, but also to the 'death' of the movement to which it pays implicit tribute (Rose, 1992:126).

Much more startling are the kinds of titles given to his work by the French surrealist painter René Magritte. These force us to question the relationship, often taken for granted, between images and words, images and what they represent. *Hegel's Holiday* is the title of a painting that depicts an open umbrella with a glass of water balanced on top. As Carter notes, 'rather than image and title being substitutable for each other, the image and its title are now equal elements' in the work (1990:162). Thus a new autonomy is achieved by words and images—images being no longer interchangeable with words, or vice versa. On the other hand, Magritte's famous painting of a pipe captioned *This is not a pipe* forces us to think about the connections between images and the objects they represent, as well as the relationship between words and the images they evoke. Both titles, moreover, establish intertextual links with works in the written media: the philosophy of Hegel and, more specifically, the philosophical *conte* entitled *Ceci n'est pas un conte* (*This is not a short story*) by the French eighteenth-century *philosophe* Denis Diderot.

Some artists, in an effort to preserve the artistic integrity of the visual image unmediated by language (or, in the case of abstract paintings, to suggest art as an autonomous, non-referential object), resort to numbers as titles (Jackson Pollock's *Number twenty-eight*) or to the designation 'untitled'. As Carter points out, the former is not neutral since it carries with it 'a set of associations with mathematics, science, impersonality and coolness' (ibid.:163). As a title, 'untitled' paradoxically suggests the impossibility of a visual experience unmediated by language, since it is only through language that the refusal to use language in the conventional way can be established.

Gallery visitors generally 'forget' that an art work is viewed within a series of embedded circumtextual frames—the physical margins of the canvas, the enclosing wooden or metal outline, the title, caption, alcove, wall, lighting effects, adjacent pictures, room, exhibition and so on. The danger of such amnesia is that we remain unaware of the mediating agencies that control our interpretation of what we see.

As for those non-material or socio-cognitive frames we have earlier included in the term 'extratextual', it must be remembered that in any act of perception we are not simply passive receivers of stimuli. We are active producers of meaning as we frame and reframe our present experience. Just as the interpreting of a written text involves more than the decoding of the individual words and the grasping of the logical connections between them, so too in making sense of a painting, a photograph or a piece of sculpture we do more than simply register colour, shape and texture. Assumptions and inferences derived from our past experience are drawn upon as we 'construct' what we see. This experience includes not only real-world knowledge of objects and situations that may be pertinent to the art object, but also familiarity with the artistic medium itself: its conventions, styles and limitations, history, practitioners, the mediating networks that govern its display and so on. One of the key roles assumed by galleries and museums, as we have seen, is to provide or to supplement this knowledge wherever possible.

Movietime: the temporal viewing frame

As David Bordwell points out, it would be surprising if movies, drawing on the interaction of visual, auditory and verbal stimuli, 'did not demand active and complex construction' on the part of the viewing subject (1985:33). In his discussion of narrative cinema, he stresses that to make sense of a film, 'the viewer must do more than perceive movement, construe images and sounds as presenting a three-dimensional world, and understand oral or written language. The viewer must take as a central cognitive goal the construction of a more or less intelligible story' (ibid.). This will involve processing what is seen and heard on the basis of the viewer's knowledge of everyday reality as well as those conventions associated with the cinematic medium itself. Interacting with this extratextual knowledge are the ways in which the film may exploit its framing potential to 'cue' the viewer's interpretation of what is on the screen.

Although James Monaco tells us that 'all the codes that operate within the frame [of a film] . . . are shared with the other pictorial arts' (1977:149), one could hardly maintain that cinematic and painted images are framed identically. Stephen Heath (1981:10) recalls Walter Benjamin's remarks on the radical difference between the experience of a spectator at a movie and the experience of a viewer in a gallery: a painting invites contemplation, says Benjamin, while a film prevents it. What Benjamin alludes to here are the constraints imposed by 'movietime'—the temporal viewing frame.

For when we watch a movie in a cinema, the temporal 'delivery' of story is totally beyond our control. As Bordwell emphasises, 'Under normal viewing circumstances, the film absolutely controls the order, frequency, and duration of the presentation of events' (1985:74). This aspect of the film-viewing experience necessarily places constraints on the perceptual and cognitive abilities of viewers. The experience of watching a narrative film thus differs fundamentally from the experience of either looking at a painting or reading a narrative text. Like gallery visitors, who can linger in front of a painting, readers have the power to pause, to reread, even to read in a different order from that prescribed by the text.

By manipulating our experience of time and space through editing, films have the potential to shape the way we respond to and interpret what we see and hear. Rapid cross-cutting to other locations in thrillers or westerns, for instance, is a common technique for generating suspense or creating ironic juxtapositions; slow-motion sequences in films like Claude Lelouche's *A Man and a Woman* or Alain Resnais' *Last Year at Marienbad* may suggest or provoke a particular state of mind; jump-cuts such as Godard uses in *Breathless* may signify disconnection and fragmentation. In the case of the freeze-frame, the sudden arresting of narrative movement foregrounds a particular image, extracting it from its context and demanding a different kind of attention. How we interpret it will depend, among other things, on where it is encountered in a film. Coming at the end of François Truffaut's *Four Hundred Blows*, the freeze-frame signifies closure, both in the literal sense of marking the end of the film, and also as a metaphor marking the passage from one stage of the young boy's life to another. When, on the other hand, it occurs unexpectedly in the middle of Truffaut's *Day for Night*, the unusual freezing of a particular character seems to invite close viewer scrutiny of his motives and actions.

Despite differences in 'movietime' and space, it is clear that the linear movement of a film aligns it with written narratives rather than paintings or other static art-forms: 'What editing and montage show is that while shot A frames the following shot B, shot B also reframes shot A, resulting in a "seeing-after-the-event" just like learning after the event' (Wilden, 1984:36). In this respect the function of the cinematic frame is much the same as the punchline in a joke: 'The punchline collapses levels, changes the context, reframes what has gone before, and remakes the structure of the story. Life is life, history is history, and jokes are jokes because in going forward we come to understand them by reading backwards' (ibid.:30). And we could add, narrative is narrative, whatever the medium—detective fiction being exemplary in requiring a reader to reframe all that has gone before from the perspective of the end.

The dry quadrilateral

Despite Monaco's insistence that the codes operating within the frame of a film are not specific to it, being shared by the other visual media, there are obvious differences worth noting here. In at least three respects, the frame for a film image is markedly different from the frame around a painted surface. To begin with, the former is limited to a fixed rectangular shape projected on to the screen— what the pioneer Russian director Sergei Eisenstein called a 'dry quadrilateral plunging into the hazards of nature's diffuseness' (1949:4). Of course this does not preclude the possibility of occasional shots that are shaped differently; for instance, 'masking' produces a circular image at the end of *10* to represent a telescopic view of Dudley Moore and Julie Andrews. Split-screen effects are also possible and often exploited in Hollywood comedies or for ironic effect as in Truffaut's *Shoot the Pianist*. Nevertheless, in size and proportions, a cinematic image must obey constraints not felt by painters.

Second, as Heath puts it, 'film destroys the ordinary laws of composition because of its moving figures which capture attention against all else' (1981:10). Since nearly every composed shot contains movement, and is quickly superseded by another shot and another in a mobile sequence, the momentary framing of screen space by the eye of the beholder bears little resemblance to the framing of any static composition. Again it is possible to subvert this principle experimentally, as Jean-Luc Godard does in *Passion* and Peter Greenaway in *The Cook, the Thief, the Wife, the Lover*. Both use 'tableau vivant' effects that allude to certain well-known paintings, playing with the potentiality for stasis and movement in these different media.

Soundtracks and other framing elements

Another basic difference between cinematic and pictorial frames is that what appears on the film screen is normally accompanied by a soundtrack. This offers opportunities for various framing relationships between image and sound, and between sound which is diegetic (part of the world of the story) and sound which is conventionally located 'off'.

Most often, the dialogue, music and other aural effects will complement and reinforce the visual effects in a fairly direct way, but not always. In her film *India Song*, Marguerite Duras disjoins soundtrack from scene: throughout, there are 'voices off' who seem to inhabit a different world from that of the non-speaking actors. In a later film, *Son nom de Vénise dans Calcutta désert*, the traditional relationship between sound and visual track is further subverted when Duras uses exactly the same soundtrack to accompany an entirely different set of visual images. In this film the silent actors of *India Song* are replaced by a series of images of decaying statues, moss-covered masonry and ruined interiors. If the viewing of this later film is framed against the earlier one, we will tend to interpret the absence of human figures as indicative of a further passing of time and the erosion of image in the memory.

As well as the interpretive potential offered by the soundtrack and the temporal dimension characteristic of the film medium, all the framing possibilities previously described in relation to painted works are also available. For instance, we make sense of films by noting their circumtextual accompaniments (stills, posters, titles, credits and the like), and by drawing intertextually on other films to construe visual quotations (a very common device in *nouvelle vague* cinema). Films, like written texts, can also be particularly resourceful in providing cues for interpretation through intratextual framing. A typical compressed example is the shot in *Beyond a Reasonable Doubt* which shows 'a police car, framed in a rearview mirror, it in turn framed by a car windshield, with the windshield in turn enclosed by the film frame' (Bordwell, 1989:140). This insistence on the visual frame is a reminder of the 'frame-up' at the heart of the story. Frequently the voyeuristic appeal of the cinematic medium itself is embedded in the film through extensive self-reference, as in *Rear Window* and *sex, lies and videotape*.

Space does not permit a summary of the large body of film theory and criticism in which technical aspects of framing are discussed at length, and to which David Bordwell (1985, 1989) offers helpful guidance. One fundamental matter worth brief comment, however, is the fact that our interpretation of a particular scene or sequence will also be affected by the position of the camera in relation to what it records. To frame something or someone in close-up rather than in a long- or medium-distance shot, to use high-angle rather than low-angle shots, will often seem to indicate a subjective attitude on the part of the director and thus to solicit a particular response from the viewer. Such interpretive assumptions are easily parodied:

> If the story of Little Red Riding Hood is told with the Wolf in close-up and Little Red Riding Hood in long-shot, the director is concerned primarily with the emotional problems of a wolf with

a compulsion to eat little girls. If Little Red Riding Hood is in close-up and the Wolf is in long-shot, the emphasis is shifted to the emotional problems of vestigial virginity in a wicked world. (Bordwell, 1989:164; cf. 175–7)

Many of the observations made in this chapter about paintings and films could also be broadly applied to aspects of other visual media such as comic strips, videoclips, photographs or television advertisements. But each art-form has its own particular set of interpretive conventions, and it is not possible here to provide a comprehensive discussion. The main general point is that any visual field, cinematic or other, is constituted by a frame. As Boris Uspensky remarks, 'In order to perceive the world of the work of art as a sign system, it is necessary (although not always sufficient) to designate its borders; it is precisely these borders which create the representation' (1973:140). But frames are not just borderlines; as we have seen, they also have the potential to carry metamessages about how to interpret what they enclose. In the next chapter we turn to some of the theorists who analyse the framing of everyday experience from this perspective.

3

Framing Experience: 'What is it that's Going on Here?'

Two theoretical affiliations

Deborah Tannen reminds us in an article on framing of the 'nearly self-evident truth' that 'in order to function in the world, people cannot treat each new person, object or event as unique and separate' (1979:137). It is only by relating new experiences to similar ones from the past that we can begin to make sense of the world. As noted in Chapter 1, framing metaphors draw attention to the fact that in order to perceive and understand anything, we must provisionally separate it from other things while also relating it to them: figure is distinguished from ground, picture from wall, medical examinations from erotic encounters and so on.

It is not surprising to find that framing metaphors are frequently invoked by researchers like Tannen in the social sciences since linguists, anthropologists, psychologists, sociologists and the many socio-cultural theorists whose interests cross disciplinary boundaries share a common concern with the problem of how we perceive and interpret human behaviour. Frame conceptions of understanding are also common in the cognitive sciences, particularly in artificial intelligence, as we will see in Chapter 4. Tannen's article (1979), with its introductory survey of frame and related metaphors across these different disciplines, represents a useful orientation to a field characterised by major differences in emphasis and usage and a sometimes confusing array of competing and overlapping terminology.

Two main theoretical affiliations should be distinguished at the outset: the 'cognitive' schemata or frames deriving from Frederick Bartlett and the 'psychological' frames deriving from Gregory Bateson. In this chapter we will focus mainly on the latter, beginning with a discussion of Bateson's influential research in this area. The rest of the chapter concentrates on those frame theorists in the social sciences whose impact has been substantial or whose application of framing metaphors has been extensive. Chapter 4 will consider the applications of frame conceptions of understanding in the cognitive area. Given the increasing tendency towards interdisciplinary convergence of interests, we should not be surprised to find that some theorists concerned with the problems of interpretation (Tannen, Gumperz and others) draw usefully on both social and cognitive science conceptions of frames.

Frames as metamessages: Gregory Bateson

Of the researchers in the social sciences who refer specifically to 'frames', most acknowledge a debt to the anthropologist Gregory Bateson. In a seminal article entitled 'A Theory of Play and Fantasy' (first published in 1955 and later incorporated in *Steps to an Ecology of Mind*, 1972), Bateson argues that an important step along the road that led to the development of human language must have been the ability to recognise and differentiate signals. Instead of responding automatically to mood signals, recognising a signal as a signal (i.e. as something that requires interpretation) indicates the capacity to communicate at different levels of abstraction.

As Bateson explains, much of the time we communicate at the level of simple denotation ('The cat is playing on the mat'). When however we refer to the language used in a statement ('The word "cat" has no fur and cannot scratch'), we are operating at a more abstract or 'metalinguistic' level of communication. *Metacommunicative* messages are more abstract still, since they are messages about (*meta*) the status of the communication itself ('My telling you that the cat was playing on the mat was only a joke'). Bateson (1972:188) points out that metacommunicative messages can be thought of as psychological 'frames' which help guide and correct the way we interpret our exchanges with others. These are the messages that tell us not what people say but what they mean:

whether a statement is intended as a joke or whether it is meant as ironic, sincere, teasing, hostile, patronising and so on.

Bateson's awareness of the evolutionary importance of these metamessages derives initially from his observation of monkeys at a zoo. Certain bodily postures and gestures in monkeys engaged in play clearly indicated 'This is play' as distinct from related but different signals which would have unequivocally denoted aggression. In a similar way metacommunicative messages are regularly exchanged in normal human interaction, enabling us to distinguish simulated from real aggression. These messages are often conveyed through non-verbal signals like facial expression and bodily stance; but given the language resources of humans, explicit verbal framing is also common. When we ask, 'Are you kidding?' or 'What does that mean?' or 'Why are you telling me this?', or when someone says, 'I'm only joking' or 'It's just a movie', we are dealing with quite explicit ways of checking our perception, or correcting the perception of others, about what is going on.

Bateson stresses that 'the ability to communicate about communication, to comment upon the meaningful actions of oneself and others, is essential for successful social intercourse' (ibid.:215). Problems are likely to occur when people fail to develop the ability to communicate in this way. On the basis of his research in the psychiatric field with schizophrenic patients, Bateson observes that it is precisely this ability that is lost in schizophrenic patients whose behaviour can be characterised as a 'metacommunicative tangle' (ibid.:195). Regularly omitting 'the frame-setting message (e.g., the phrase "as if")'—presumably because he cannot make the necessary framing discriminations himself—the schizophrenic patient fails to signal the differences between metaphorical and literal statements. This is similar to the situation of the dreamer, who is rarely conscious of the dreaming frame. As Bateson comments: 'The absence of metacommunicative framing which was noted in the case of dreams is characteristic of the waking communications of the schizophrenic' (ibid.:190).

Bateson hypothesises about the origins of such a condition, concluding that certain early 'learning' contexts favour the development of what are presumably hereditary potentialities. Focusing on the family unit, and in particular on the patient's relationship with the mother-figure, he theorises that schizophrenia develops out of the frustrations generated by the experience of a perpetual 'double bind'. This is a situation in which the patient feels compelled to obey contradictory messages which create a habitual 'no-win' position for the patient, a kind of communicative 'trap' from which he cannot escape (ibid.:201–27).

Implicit in Bateson's analysis of the typical double-bind situation is the way in which meanings are controlled through frame manipulation by the mother. By a tactic of constantly reframing the child's communication and behaviour ('You don't mean that, do you?'), and explicitly but falsely representing her own ('I'm doing this for your own good'), the mother undermines the child's ability to detect the underlying metamessage of ambivalence or hostility. An accurate reading of the mother's metamessages would result in the punishment of hostile withdrawal by the mother. So too would an inaccurate reading, since a loving response to the mother's simulated affection would reactivate the mother's fear or hostility and the same kind of punishment would follow. In these circumstances it is not difficult to understand how the development of metacommunicative skills, which might enable the 'victim' to comment on the situation and offer a possible escape from the trap, is totally inhibited.

The double bind is clear: in order to survive with the mother, the child 'must falsely discriminate his own internal messages as well as falsely discriminate the messages of others' (ibid.:214). He therefore grows up, Bateson hypothesises, 'unskilled in his ability to communicate about communication and, as a result, unskilled in determining what people really mean and unskilled in expressing what he really means, which is essential for normal relationships' (ibid.:216).

It is significant that the mother's motives are not really explored by Bateson; nor is he interested in investigating the complex interrelationships which (he acknowledges) characterise family structures. This one-sidedness is evident in the example he gives of a situation in which he himself was involved when he took a schizophrenic patient home to visit the patient's mother. Struck by the 'model' aspect of the mother's immaculate house and garden, he decided, while filling in time during the patient's visit, to do something to change 'this set-up'. 'What and how could I communicate?', he wonders. The solution, he decides, is to introduce into the home environment 'something that was both beautiful and untidy'. With this in mind Bateson chooses a bunch of gladioli which he presents as a gift to the mother framed by the words just quoted. Her response? 'Oh! Those are not untidy flowers. As each one withers, you can snip it off ' (ibid.:198–9).

Bateson comments that this is a false interpretation of his message, since her statement put him in the position 'of having apologized when in fact I had not. That is, she took my message and reclassified it. She changed the label which indicated what sort of message it was, and that is, I believe, what she does all the time' (ibid.: 199). This may well be the case, but Bateson, disregarding the context of the exchange, seems blind to the power-play going on here between the powerful doctor figure and the relatively powerless mother whom he positions as culpable in some unspecified way for having a tidy house. The implications of this covert message of rebuke must be obvious to her, given the mental condition of her son and the authority vested in the doctor treating him. A counter-framing rejection of such positioning is not necessarily pathological in view of the double bind Bateson has (unwittingly?) created for her.

Despite Bateson's theoretical acknowledgement of the asymmetry of the power relations involved in family and therapeutic contexts, he seems peculiarly forgetful of the way it operates in his own practice, at least on this particular occasion (ibid.:237). In fact, the struggle to control the frame—which is a struggle to control meaning—remains an issue he chooses to allude to rather than to explore in his discussions of the learning contexts constituted by family and therapeutic environments. With his focus firmly on the way in which one party is positioned by another (himself in the flowers episode, the patient in his theorising) he recognises, but largely brackets, the broader context in which these relationships are embedded. His analysis of this exchange also suggests a reversion to a belief in a simple transmission model of human communication whereby messages are sent and received in an unproblematic way. There appears to be no acknowledgement of the possibility of 'noise' in the system produced by the asymmetry in power between sender and receiver. Bateson's own metamessage of rebuke is therefore simply left out of account.

Reframing experience

Not surprisingly, individual rather than family therapy is the treatment endorsed by Bateson. Given his view of the origins of schizophrenia, it follows that the therapist's role will be to try to change the patient's 'metacommunicative habits'—his abnormal use of frames—by manipulating them. The therapist does this in that special semiotic space constituted by the therapeutic session which, ironically, is itself 'an analogue of the frame-setting message which the schizophrenic is unable to achieve' (ibid.:190–2).

In his discussion of play and fantasy, Bateson elaborates on the similarities between the framing of play and therapy:

> Both occur within a delimited psychological frame, a spatial and temporal bounding of a set of interactive messages. In both play and therapy, the messages have a special and peculiar relationship to a more concrete or basic reality. Just as the pseudocombat of play is not real combat, so also the pseudolove and pseudohate of therapy are not real love or hate. The 'transfer' is discriminated from real love and hate by signals invoking the psychological frame; and indeed it is this frame which permits the transfer to reach its full intensity and to be discussed between patient and therapist. (ibid.:191)

Although Bateson, writing in 1955, lacks a semiotic theory to explain how particular ways of framing experience produce different meanings, a recognition of this principle is implicit in his examples. As we saw in Chapters 1 and 2, certain situations or spaces institutionalised by society can be seen as constituting semiotic fields within which events and relationships signify differently. These 'larger contexts', to use Bateson's terminology, like the therapeutic or teaching situation, ritual and ceremonial occasions, theatres, museums and art galleries, may work to change the sign or the mode of a particular message.

The therapist can therefore be the agent for changes in the sign of a given message. Using a slightly different analogy, Bateson compares the way in which a particular frame transforms the meaning of what it encloses to those segments of equations or 'messages' which mathematicians put in brackets. The tenor of these 'messages' can be altered by the addition of an operator outside the brackets. The therapist is just such an operator, working on past material even at a distance of many years. What is central therefore to Bateson's discussion of 'psychological' (or perceptual) frames is their dynamic potential for, or vulnerability to, change. Unlike material frames, psychological frames are not stable structures, but 'labile', provisional perceptions, open to (therapeutic) intervention as well as to (maternal) manipulation. In Bateson's view, it follows then that the therapist's task, ironically similar to the mother's, consists in manipulating or reframing past and present material in ways that are deemed to be more appropriate to the patient's situation.

It is important to recognise the framework within which Bateson himself is operating in his research in this area. As we have seen, his view of schizophrenia emerges from a particular theory of learning and communication. Defining it as a communication disorder, he traces its origins to a response to a particular stimulus— the learning environment provided by the double bind. Other views of the etiology of schizophrenia developed within the framework of a different theory—of, say, the role of a particular chemical imbalance in triggering schizophrenic behaviour—would necessarily imply therapeutic intervention of a very different kind.

(For a more recent example of the ways in which therapeutic 'reframing' of past events is currently practised, see Bandler and Grindler, 1979, 1982.)

Frame analysis: Erving Goffman

By far the most detailed development of a theory of framing to date is Erving Goffman's *Frame Analysis: An Essay on the Organization of Experience* (1974). This book deserves extensive discussion here in view of its broad scope and theoretical importance. Starting with the question which Goffman assumes individuals face when attending to any situation: 'What is it that's going on here?' his book 'attempts to limn out a framework that could be appealed to for the answer' (1974:8). His analysis of the question draws on research in many fields—psychology, linguistics, sociology—acknowledging a particular debt to Bateson's paper on play and fantasy and to the metaphors of 'frame' and 'brackets' which he borrows from him.

As Goffman's statement of aims suggests, he is concerned in his analyses not with the macro-structures that organise social life but with the micro-level of individual experience and how it is organised. This is not meant, he assures us, to reflect any convictions about the primacy of individual experience, but rather the simple desire to focus his analysis on 'matters that are second' (ibid.). Goffman's assumption here is that these two levels—the individual and the social—are independent of each other and therefore open to separate analysis. Indeed he asserts that 'social organisation and social structure' can be studied 'without reference to frame at all' (ibid.:13). Fascinating as much of Goffman's discussion is, such an exclusive emphasis on the individual's organisation of experience, in isolation from the broader socio-cultural frameworks within which it is embedded, constitutes the major weakness of his approach. This issue will be taken up more fully later.

As he states it, his aim 'is to isolate the basic frameworks available in our society for making sense of experience and to analyze the special vulnerabilities to which these frames of reference are subject' (ibid.:10). The sorts of vulnerabilities that Goffman has in mind are connected with the fact that for him, like Bateson, frames are not stable structures which unambiguously demarcate strips of experience. As he points out, there is a sense in which opposing supporters at a football match do not experience the same game (any more than student and teacher experience the same tutorial class) (ibid.:9). Experience is always subject to (re)organisation or (re)framing according to different interests and points of view, and this makes possible various disturbances to our perception of 'what it is that's going on'. As Goffman puts it:

> I start with the fact that from an individual's point of view, while one thing may momentarily appear to be what is really going on, in fact what is actually happening is plainly a joke, or a dream, or an accident, or a mistake, or a misunderstanding, or a

deception, or a theatrical performance, and so forth . . . Attention will be directed to what it is about our sense of what is going on that makes it so vulnerable to the need for these various re-readings. (ibid.:10)

At the core of his project, therefore, is an emphasis on the provisionality of the interpreter's view of what is going on. Goffman's aim is to account not only for the variety of interpretations generated by shifting perceptions but also for the ways in which those frame-setting cues which guide and correct our interpretation are vulnerable to manipulation and contestation. Frame contestation, however, is less fully developed in his study.

As a preliminary move in his frame analysis, Goffman distinguishes two kinds of 'primary' frameworks for interpreting experience: the natural and the social. Reference to primary frameworks provides a first answer to the question 'What is it that's going on here?'. 'Natural' frameworks enable us to isolate those occurrences which are seen as 'undirected, unoriented, unanimated, unguided, purely physical', while 'social' frameworks enable us to distinguish events which incorporate 'the will, aim, and controlling effort of an intelligence, a live agency, the chief one being the human being' (ibid.:22). Consensus even at this primary level is not something that Goffman takes for granted. Tensions also exist at the margins or boundaries that distinguish one primary frame from another. The question of a culture's 'framework of frameworks' (the belief systems or ideologies within which it operates) is a complicating factor, but one which nevertheless remains outside Goffman's own frame of reference (ibid.:27).

Combat or play? A question of keying

According to Goffman, not all frameworks are primary, since not all frameworks confer meaning in and by themselves. In his discussion of Bateson's theory of play he makes this clear: play activity among animals has meaning, he says, only because it

is closely patterned after something that already has a meaning in its own terms—in this case fighting, a well-known type of guided doing . . . Bitinglike behavior occurs, but no one is seriously bitten. In brief, there is a transcription or transposition . . . of a strip of fighting behavior into a strip of play. (ibid.:41)

The transformation of one activity, which already carries a certain meaning, into something modelled on this activity but interpreted quite differently involves a process of transcription which Goffman terms *keying*. As he comments, a rough analogy with music is intended.

In the area of human behaviour keys abound, because humans not only play at fighting but can also fantasise a fight, stage one in accordance with a script, ritualise fighting in various ways, write a fictional account of one, and so on. It is easy to see how the concept of keying—a kind of second-order activity—becomes central to Goffman's frame analysis since, although the observed activity may scarcely differ from its model, certain signals completely alter our perception of its meaning. Keying thus 'performs a crucial role in determining what we think is really going on' (ibid.:45) and includes such activities as make-believe, sporting contests, ceremonials, practices and rehearsals, role-playing, demonstrations, exhibitions and what Goffman terms 'regroundings'. Regroundings refer to activities which are performed for reasons or motives 'felt to be radically different from those that govern ordinary actors' (ibid.:74). The example Goffman offers is charity work, when some 'upper middle-class matron' or member of royalty offers her services behind the counter of a stall at a fête, thus performing a role that is similar to play-acting.

One important way in which keyings differ from primary frameworks is that the latter are seldom explicitly invoked or acknowledged. Keyings, on the other hand, promote the need for confirmation about what is going on by more or less explicit reference ('Are they fighting or only playing?', 'Is that a ladder or an art work?'). Goffman also points out that cues in the form of spatial and temporal 'brackets' help establish a frame for the transformed activity. In a life-drawing class, for instance, the aesthetic frame helps to establish the status of a naked body as an object for artistic representation rather than erotic contemplation. As in the case of gynaecological examinations, discussed in Chapter 1, conventions operate within this frame, prohibiting touch and the catching of the model's eye or any other communication during the (temporally bounded) period of the modelling session. Violations of these boundaries would have the effect of weakening the artistic frame and its capacity 'to preclude other readings' (ibid.:78).

Also common, as Goffman points out, is the *rekeying* of an already keyed transformation. This creates the potential for an endless series of complicated and sometimes playful modulations of primary material. Such keyed transformations are particularly common in literature, film and theatrical performance, since these are already modelled on primary frameworks which have meaning in their own right. Examples abound. The second episode of an Australian TV drama series called *Seven Deadly Sins* represented, within the frame of an acting workshop, the improvisation of a triangular situation involving a man, his wife and the 'other woman'. This in turn served to key a 'real-life' situation within the drama, itself ironically framed by the rehearsal and performance of a play keying a similar situation. If that seems confusing, there is more: the whole episode represented a rekeying of a keying—the first episode in the series—from which it quoted actual dialogue as well as the basic triangular situation. *Rekeying* does its work then not on a primary framework but on a (re)keying or transformation of that material.

One of the intriguing aspects of that particular episode of *Seven Deadly Sins* is the fact that the theatrical frame for the opening scene—a rehearsal of a play within the play—remains invisible until the camera pulls back to reveal the proscenium arch and stage. And yet right from the beginning, certain cues (type of dialogue, gesture, tone and elocutionary manner) suggest to the television audience the 'rekeyed' nature of what is going on. As Goffman remarks in respect of another similar example, no matter how complicated the levels of transformation or rekeying involved, 'while watching the show, the audience can follow along and read off what is happening by attending to the relevant *framing cues*' (ibid.:186).

A second kind of reworking of a primary model can occur. Goffman calls this 'fabrication', since it involves the deliberate manipulation of frames (out of benign or exploitative motives) to create false belief about what is going on. In these situations the victims of the deception are unaware of the constructedness of the frame containing the activity in which they are involved. According to Goffman, affects such as suspicion (the feeling that a frame has been constructed of which we are unaware) and doubt (hesitation over which frame to apply to a particular experience) are 'generated *by the very way in which experience is framed*' and may therefore be triggered independently of any actual frame manipulation by others (ibid.:122).

Out-of-frame activity

Subordinate to certain kinds of 'main-frame' activity, especially those social activities that are collectively organised and constitute an official focus of attention, are other goings-on in the same location. These are what Goffman refers to as 'out-of-frame' events, events which participants in the main action are normally required to 'disattend' (ibid.:210ff). Familiar examples would include the ushering of people to their seats during the opening sequence of a film, the boys retrieving balls on the sidelines at a tennis tournament, a waiter dropping a tray on his way to the kitchen, or a soldier fainting on the parade ground. Anyone involved in out-of-frame activity is a kind of 'non-person' performing duties as unobtrusively as possible. Goffman does not explore the question of social hierarchy usually reflected in the division of labour on such occasions, but focuses instead on the fact that attention to the 'disattend track' generally indicates boredom or resistance to the 'main-frame' activity. One of the main functions of out-of-frame activity of this kind is of course that it serves to establish and reinforce what it is happening inside the frame. Regulative or directional cues, like punctuation, are other kinds of signals which, while seldom attended to specifically, nevertheless closely organise what they frame.

The 'actors' on such occasions sometimes choose to go out-of-frame during performance for a variety of reasons and with a variety of effects. Lecturers may pause in their delivery to acknowledge the late entry of a student, to challenge the inattention of a member of the audience or to comment ironically on the formality of the whole procedure. They may also pause to take a sip of water or blow their nose. If any such out-of-frame activity is prolonged, however, actors run the risk of finding it difficult to re-establish the frame. Pertinent here is Uspensky's comment (1973:138) that whereas the intrusion of art into life may change the borders of artistic space without damage to them, the reverse situation—life intruding into art—succeeds in destroying the frame. As examples he cites physical attacks on paintings and the murder by a medieval audience of an actor playing Judas.

In written texts, out-of-frame activity can take the form of footnotes or stage directions (part of the 'directional' track) or such typographical conventions as parentheses and brackets which enable the writer 'to comment in another voice—another role and another frame—on his own text' (ibid.:227 ff). An editorial frame can also be inserted alongside the authorial one.

Frame-breaking

As we have seen, out-of-frame activity is intended to be treated by others as peripheral to the main event, something to be 'disattended'. 'Going out of frame', however, presupposes an activity under the control of the main player(s) which is not intended to be ignored. Such breaks in the frame applied to an activity are often reflexive and deliberately draw attention to the frame itself. Direct reader-address in narrative, or asides and soliloquies in drama, are familiar examples of frame-breaking in literary texts. Frame-breaks are not exclusive to written texts. As Goffman comments, 'every setting has its moments when participants may momentarily break frame', but minor frame-breaks simply work to 'ensure the continuity and viability of the established frame' (ibid.:382).

Frame-breaks are often used by a writer or performer to maintain interest at critical points in the performance. In Goffman's view, self-referencing frame-breaks fall into this category, since they allow attention to be drawn away from the main 'story' to the framing mechanism which works to maintain it. Such breaks are common in the plays of Luigi Pirandello and Samuel Beckett and in many postmodern texts. In the case of self-referential movies, Goffman takes to task the French director Jean-Luc Godard for what he calls 'frame-discrediting' breaks. Susan Sontag had observed that to include in a film a shot of a clapper board (as Godard does in *La Chinoise*), or of the cameraman filming the sequence, is to conjure up in the viewer's mind another cameraman shooting the scene showing the cameraman, and another person holding the clapper board for that scene, and so on in a dizzying series of shots. Goffman regards this sort of thing as an act of bad faith. When anyone tries to draw attention to the frame that is being employed, he claims, 'the posture he thereby assumes inevitably denies awareness of the frame in which *that* posture is struck. He adds that 'this holds as well for one whose intent is to direct attention to this effect' (ibid.:404). This is a strange conclusion to draw, since Goffman agrees with Sontag that 'one immediately imagines' the framing gesture which incorporates the framed one. Self-reflexive gestures of this kind (like Goffman's in his own preface) are surely intended to foreground the mediated or framed nature of cinematic (and all other) experience.

Insider's folly

Goffman is particularly interested in the vulnerability of experience to deception and illusion. It is obvious that special opportunities 'for those who would deceive' can be generated by framing tricks of one kind or another (ibid.:463). There is, for example, a common swindle which works by framing what is going on as a conspiracy to entrap someone else. According to Goffman, when people are involved in deceiving someone else, their ability to maintain sceptical awareness of the venture itself and of their fellow conspirators is much reduced (ibid.:474). This is the 'folly' associated with the insider position. A typical case quoted by Goffman involves a 'bank official' telephoning a depositor to enlist help in trapping a dishonest teller. The depositor is asked to withdraw his savings, after being assured that the banknotes have been marked and will be taken by the officials as evidence against the teller. Neither the fake officials nor the real banknotes are ever seen again!

In this analysis, Goffman cites a certain kind of reflexive framebreak common in theatrical texts—the play within the play—as 'the most familiar exploitation of insider's folly' (ibid.). Such devices, he implies, serve to anchor more firmly the frame of what we are experiencing by, in effect, making it less visible in relation to another foregrounded frame. In Goffman's view, this works as a 'trap for inducing involvement and belief' (ibid.). Spectators 'find that in being eased out of belief in the play within the play, they are automatically eased into belief concerning the play that contains the play within the play' (ibid.:475). What Goffman seems to overlook here is the fact that such devices are bound to operate differently in the 'keyed' realm of the theatrical frame. Unlike the situation exploited by the con man, audiences are aware of the frame in which they are co-operating and are therefore not really 'insiders' in the same sense. Moreover recognition of literary 'tricks' will usually have the effect of drawing us into a relationship of pleasurable collusion with the 'trickster'.

The frame paradox revisited

The boundaries between what is inside the frame and what lies outside it are not always as clearly demarcated as some of these examples might seem to suggest. As Goffman implies in his discussion of frame-breaks, frames are labile structures which are subject to collapse and violation, being especially vulnerable at the margins. Indeed, as we have seen, any discussion of the borderline between the frame and its surround leads to apparent paradox. Goffman makes this point quite strongly:

> Activity framed in a particular way—especially collectively organized social activity—is often marked off from the ongoing flow of surrounding events by a special set of boundary markers or brackets of a conventionalized kind . . . These markers, like the wooden frame of a picture, are presumably neither part of the content of activity proper nor part of the world outside the activity but rather both inside and outside, a paradoxical condition . . . not to be avoided just because it cannot be thought about clearly. (ibid.: 252)

What Goffman is stressing here is the double-edged quality of frames: that is, frames function both as part of the structure of what they enclose (at their inner edge) and (at the outer edge or rim of the frame) part of the 'outside' world against which the enclosed text or activity is framed. As John Frow reminds us, frames are of course 'unitary, neither inside nor outside', any distinction between inner and outer edges being no more than a fiction 'to express the "thickness" of the frame, its duality as a component of structure and a component of situation' (1986:222). The boundary-markers or brackets that define the limits of the 'theatrical frame' function both as part of that make-believe experience and as a way of marking it off from the reality of everyday life. 'This operation of exclusion' (from reality) is at the same time 'also an inclusion of the text' (or activity) 'in this alien space' (ibid.). Thus, as Frow notes, 'the frame does not simply separate an inside from an outside but unsettles the distinction between the two' (ibid.:223).

Frames as 'brackets'

Such boundary-markers, often naturalised to the point of invisibility, none the less set up expectations, creating a mood or particular kind of attention appropriate to the framed activity. The convention of dimmed lights and the rising curtain, formulae like 'Once upon a time', the use of a gavel to call a meeting to order, the tuning up of the orchestra before a concert, the bringing of the menu in a restaurant—all are opening markers of ceremonies with which we are very familiar. Reliance on opening and closing conventions to establish the frame of an activity, however, can be playfully exploited in various ways. Goffman cites musical examples, including the way in which Karlheinz Stockhausen's *Hymnen* begins with static, 'a classic non-performance sound' (1974:392–3). What the audience takes to be activity outside the performance space of a concert, and constitutive of it, must be reframed as part of that concert space. Such 'tricks' serve to blur the boundaries between performance and non-performance space, to problematise what lies inside or outside the frame.

Manipulations of either the opening or closing brackets of a theatrical or ceremonial performance draw audience attention to the conventional nature of these cues. Goffman gives many theatrical examples from the theatre of the absurd (which he suggests renaming the 'theatre of frames', ibid.:399) and also a play which begins with 'real musicians practising onstage and characters in the guise of the play's director and author entering from the audience aisles, talking as if things had not yet begun' (ibid.:401).

What is apparent throughout Goffman's analysis is the fundamental precariousness of the frame and the various ways in which pre-emptive control over its maintenance may be exerted by the writer/performer in charge of the proceedings. But frames are also vulnerable to attack 'from below', the most obvious examples of which are heckling or similar acts of disattention or disturbance from the audience. Such breaking down of the boundaries between audience and performers can of course be incorporated into or indeed constitute part of the show as, for example, in melodrama. Other ceremonies exert strict control over performer–audience communication. This is the case in many sports, where conventional etiquette requires that players ignore applause, boos or catcalls from the spectators (ibid.:416).

Errors of framing

Goffman devotes a substantial section of his analysis to the ways in which our framing of events can lead to error, ambiguities and frame disputes. Determining the 'correct' meaning of an event is not what is at issue here, but rather the question of which of the various frameworks available it is appropriate to apply in a particular situation (ibid.:304). For to misread an event is not to commit an error of the type involved in adding up a column of figures; it is to be wrongly oriented towards an event, often for a considerable period of time, sometimes forever. Such misperception can involve 'a perspective that is itself radically inapplicable, which will itself establish a set, a whole grammar of expectations, that will not work' (ibid.:309). The jealous lover, the very young or naive observer and the paranoid personality will often be predisposed to misread things. Comic situations can arise when, having misconstrued what is happening, people find themselves in an inappropriate relationship to those events. Shakespeare's comedies, involving 'spectacular misalignments to the world' (ibid.:444) over the span of several acts, are dramatically heightened examples of such errors. 'Miskeyings' are also common as when, for example, television viewers are unaware that what they are watching is not a play but a play within a play.

When more than one way of framing an event is possible, *frame disputes* may arise. Sexual harassment cases, for example, frequently involve conflicting interpretations of interpersonal relations in the work place. In these cases the excuse of *misframing* may be invoked as a way of avoiding responsibility when unacceptable behaviour is publicly denounced or legal sanctions are brought to bear against it. Claims regarding 'keying' can also be made in disputes over frame where, for instance, somebody tries to represent an action as non-serious so as to diminish responsibility for it, claiming that they were 'only joking'. More complicated is the type of behaviour which involves the simultaneous maintenance of two contradictory positions. This results in a kind of 'bad faith' reminiscent of Bateson's 'double bind', which Goffman categorises as a variety of *frame trap*. 'The method is to employ careful ambiguities or a tone that can be claimed to signal either a joking unseriousness or a face-value intent', he notes. 'Any tendency on the recipient's part to elect one of the interpretations is checked by an act that gives strength to the alternative reading. A technique, in effect, for keeping someone on the hook' (ibid.:387–8).

Another kind of frame trap is question-begging: 'Have you stopped beating your wife?'. More complicated examples arise, however, in situations like the therapeutic session, where attempts to 'clear the frame' serve merely to reinforce it. Concepts like patient 'resistance' can be invoked by therapists whenever their patients disagree with their interpretation or the course of their treatment. Goffman thus ironically defines 'resistance' as 'a psychic condition which has the miraculous power of tranforming verbal disagreement with the therapist into evidence that the therapist is right' (ibid.:482).

Accusations of *frame-ups* are also common in frame disputes. These involve claims that others have deliberately arranged events so that someone appears in a bad or a criminal light (ibid.:334). Higher-order frame disputes generally ensue. Such situations—since doubt tends to breed doubt—may give rise to a number of possible readings, none of which can be established definitively. As Goffman notes, 'these possibilities are endemic to framing, constituting a fundamental feature, a fundamental slippage, in the organization of experience' (ibid.:323). Kurosawa's film *Rashomon*, with its multiple and conflicting versions of the same 'rape' sequence, is a cinematic illustration of this aspect of human experience.

Less common are disputes regarding what Goffman calls 'the framing arrangements available in the community' (ibid.:336). Disputes in this area are generally referred to expert adjudicators such as official courts of appeal in law, scientific and medical opinion and the like. As Goffman puts it, these institutions are concerned not just with maintaining standards: 'they are also concerned with maintaining clarity with respect of framing' (ibid.:337). Although Goffman mentions these larger frameworks, an analysis of the kinds of social control they exert is outside the scope of his analysis.

Context revisited

Contextual cues may also provide support for a particular reading of what it is that's going on. Indeed, Goffman defines context in precisely these terms: 'immediately available events which are compatible with one frame understanding and incompatible with others' (ibid.:441). By stressing the priority of the act of framing to determine what can be regarded as constituting the contextual field, Goffman alludes to the problem of circularity we mentioned in chapter one: the *prior* framing of a field so as to establish what in the first place *is* the context for a given event. Goffman also alludes to the role of what we have called *extratextual* frames when he states that while 'it is true that context helps to rule out unintended meanings and suppress misunderstanding . . . the immediate surround could not have this power apart from the sophistication— the cultural competence—of interpreters' (ibid.:496). Cultural *incompetence* therefore constitutes a further source of potential framing error.

In the case of written texts, generic markers or cues perform a similar how-to-read or metacommunicative function, since they help to establish a frame for our understanding of what is going on. Whether we read Alex Haley's *Roots* as history or fiction is largely a matter of how the text frames itself. Cries of 'hoax' occur only when evidence is produced which persuades us that the book misrepresents its relationship to historical truth. In the light of new evidence, we may be induced to reframe it as fiction rather than genealogical history, and in doing so we bring to our reading a different set of expectations, a different kind of involvement with the text.

It is obvious then that the absence of any framing indications is profoundly disorienting, as any listener who has tuned in mid-programme to the radio will have experienced. Deliberate manipulation or violation of framing conventions can also occur, a famous example being Orson Welles's radio broadcast of H. G. Wells's *The War of the Worlds* (ibid.:365). Listeners who were presumably waiting for the play to begin were led astray by the 'invisibility' of the show's theatrical frame. Without any indication that the show had begun, a weather report was given followed by a musical interlude during which a series of station interruptions by actors playing the part of radio announcers introduced the play. It appears that many listeners were deceived into thinking that war had really broken out. Prefaces, misleading titles and other circumtextual frames can induce a false set of expectations in the case of written texts, as Chapter 5 will show.

Framing Goffman

If we ask what it is that's going on in Goffman's own analysis of frames, the answer might be an attempt (presumably unconscious) to maintain the invisibility of the socio-political frameworks that make certain perceptions *possible* in the organisation of our personal experience. In other words there are always limits on who can say what, under what circumstances, and to whom. Asymmetries in the power relations between people, certain institutional settings, the gender, age, education or ethnicity of the participants in an exchange of this kind—these are all factors of which we may be only partially aware, but which nevertheless affect not only how we interpret experience but also how, when or even whether we can give expression to our interpretations.

As noted earlier, what limits Goffman's analysis of frames is his restrictive focus on the 'micro-level' of individual experience. No connection is established between the quasi-invisibility of frames and the politics of frame manipulation at the macro-level of our experience. For Goffman, frames are vulnerable to manipulation by con men, swindlers, hoaxers and practical jokers. Those broader socio-political frames (gender, race, ethnicity, class, and the various institutional frames) that control the range of meanings available to us are referred to only incidentally, if at all. The problem is that by omitting a critical account of such wider frameworks, he helps to foster an illusion of individual autonomy.

Goffman's approach, as he himself concedes, has politically conservative implications (ibid.:14). Whether homosexuality is framed as a 'sin' or a 'crime' or a 'disease' or as a genetically determined 'orientation', the classification will have far-reaching social and political consequences for individual homosexuals. An awareness of the various institutional frameworks (religious, legal, medical) which confer labels on human sexual behaviour, and of the ways in which such behaviour has been variously framed in the past, leaves the way open to challenge and change. Changes in how we frame difference can only proceed from an awareness of how difference gets framed in the first place, and for this we need the corrective of some kind of historical perspective. Despite occasional references to past practices, such a perspective is lacking in Goffman's analysis.

Since those who would frame others are also vulnerable to readerly misgivings about the limits of their own analysis, perhaps the penultimate word should be Goffman's: 'This book will have weaknesses enough in the areas it claims to deal with; there is no need to find limitations in regard to what it does not set out to cover' (ibid.:13). Or is there? Goffman's attempt here to specify in what ways his own work may and may not be framed raises important questions about the politics of interpretation which we shall address in our final chapter.

Framing conversation: Deborah Tannen

Whereas Goffman devotes only one chapter of his book to the analysis of talk, Deborah Tannen (drawing on the work of Goffman and Bateson as well as linguists such as Lakoff and Gumperz) has written a number of books, some scholarly, some popular, which focus exclusively on the question of how people interpret meaning in everyday conversation. With her emphasis on 'conversational style', on 'how' one says something rather than 'what' one says, framing issues inevitably arise.

As some of Tannen's titles suggest (*You Just Don't Understand*, 1991, and *That's Not What I Meant!*, 1992), what interest her are the misunderstandings that can occur in conversation. These she attributes not so much to attitudinal problems in the relationship between the participants as to misinterpretations based on differences in conversational 'styles'. Starting from the premise that there is no 'one-to-one relationship between linguistic form and meaning', Tannen stresses that 'the same linguistic and, inseparably, paralinguistic form can have different meanings depending on the speaker (who is saying it) and the context (how the speaker perceives the situation and the relationships among participants)' (1984:76). Determining which meaning is intended by the speaker presupposes an ability to interpret the linguistic and other framing devices that 'signal how an utterance is meant' (ibid.:9). Differences in social or cultural background can result in a failure to recognise, or a misrecognition of, such cues. Consider the following example:

Husband: 'Let's drop in on Oliver tonight.'
Wife: 'Why?'
Husband: 'All right, we don't have to go.' (Tannen, 1992:8–9)

Clearly the husband interprets his wife's 'why?' not as a request for information about the purpose of the visit but as an indication of her reluctance to visit. In doing so, he is responding not to what his wife actually says but to what he thinks his wife means, that is, her attitude to his suggestion. Following Bateson's view of frames as metacommunication, Tannen distinguishes between what we say—the message—and what we mean—the 'metamessage':

Information conveyed by the meanings of words is the message. What is communicated about relationships—attitudes towards each other, the occasion and what we are saying—is the metamessage. And it's metamessages we react to most strongly . . . comments like 'It's not what you said but the way that you said it' or . . . 'Obviously it's not nothing; something's wrong' are responses to metamessages of talk. (ibid.:13)

There are of course many occasions when people *do* mean more than they actually say, using various kinds of indirectness to convey metamessages to others. Since it hints rather than directly states how we feel about something, indirectness has the advantage of 'testing the interactional waters before committing too much—a natural way of balancing our needs with the needs of others' (ibid.:60). Such hints may be conveyed by facial expression, gesture, posture or other forms of body 'language'. These are generally referred to as 'paralinguistic' cues because they exist outside and alongside (*para*) verbal language. But such hints may also be conveyed by the prosodic features of utterances like pitch variation (rising or falling intonation), loudness and softness, pausing and pacing. As Tannen points out, these are ways of framing the words we speak to convey metamessages of anger, excitement, aggression, sincerity, irony, sarcasm, uncertainty, impatience, teasing, earnestness and so on.

In Tannen's view, it is important to recognise how these framing devices operate, since differences in the way we use them account for many of the misunderstandings that occur in our conversations with others. Normally, since such signals or cues are largely determined by socio-cultural custom (and automatically accompany whatever we have to say), we seldom employ them or respond to them consciously. Often it is only when they fail to work that we develop any awareness of them at all.

Such failure is common in cross-cultural communication. Drawing on the work of the anthropological linguist John Gumperz (1982a) and his colleagues, Tannen points out that Indian speakers are often thought by their British conversational partners to be angry because of their habit of speaking louder than is conventional in British society: 'The problem is exacerbated when an Indian speaker is trying to get the floor. Whereas a typical British strategy for getting the floor is to repeat a sentence beginning until it is heard, a typical Asian way of getting the floor is to utter the sentence beginning in a louder voice' (Tannen, 1992:32; see also Gumperz, 1982b).

There are also purely linguistic signals that interact with these paralinguistic cues, such as choice of vocabulary, type of utterance, levels of formality, type of address, and use of certain pronouns like 'we' instead of 'I'. How one deals with the differences in turn-taking which give rise to problems of conversational overlap and interruption, as well as differences in such things as speed of delivery (pacing and pausing habits) may also convey quite different meanings from what we think we intend. Tannen (1984) has made a detailed analysis of cross-cultural differences at work in a dinner party conversation, and has shown more recently (1991) how differences in conversational style between males and females reveal isssues of dominance and control.

Your frame or mine?

Signals and devices like those discussed above 'serve to frame our utterances through metamessages about what we think is going on, what we're doing when we say something, and our attitudes towards what we say and the people we say it to' (Tannen, 1992:63). Here Tannen draws attention to the ways we establish 'the *footing* that frames our relationships to each other' (ibid.:64), a term she borrows from Goffman (1981). As the following example suggests, metamessages not only identify an activity but also indicate 'what position the speaker is assuming in the activity' and what position we are being assigned by that speaker:

> For example, if you talk to others as if you were a teacher and they were your students, they may perceive that your way of talking frames you as condescending or pedantic. If you talk to others as if you were a student seeking help and explanations, they may perceive you as insecure, incompetent, or naive. Our reactions to what others say or do are often sparked by how we feel we are being framed. (Tannen, 1991:33–4)

Since we do not always feel comfortable with the way we are positioned by others, the problem of changing and challenging frames inevitably arises:

> Sometimes we feel put down by others' apparent kindness because their concern entails a subtle and unflattering reframing of our worlds. When stated and perceived frames conflict, we feel hamstrung, caught in what Bateson called a double bind. To deal with reframing that makes us uncomfortable, we can tackle the problem directly, or indirectly, by counterframing. Many of us instinctively stay in the frames set by others; some of us instinctively resist them. (Tannen, 1992:64)

Resistance is never easy, however, given the disadvantages of indirectness; for as Tannen points out, it is much more difficult to challenge how something was framed than to challenge its

propositional content (ibid.:71). Moreover, metamessages are sometimes missed, ignored, denied or misinterpreted. Disputes commonly arise when one partner asserts/believes that the other is
'reading too much into' a statement or situation.

Metamessages and meta-metamessages

Alluding to the quasi-invisibility of frames in a subsection entitled
'Frames go nameless', Tannen also states that 'since framing, by its
very nature, is signalled indirectly, naming the frame invokes a
different one' (ibid.:65). As an example she gives the situation set
up by the parent who announces to an adolescent son, 'I'd like to
have a little chat with you'. Tannen points out that 'The son, who
may respond, "What have I done now?" expects something far
weightier than a "little chat", which can only come about by the way,
when it's not labelled . . . When all is well, frames do their work
unnoticed and unnamed' (ibid.:65). One might add here that
equally, when all is *not* well, frames do their work unnoticed and
unnamed, as with so many of the ideological or 'commonsense'
assumptions we bring to experience.

Examples that seem to endorse Tannen's view are not difficult to
find. Comments such as, 'Now I'm going to ask a stupid question'
or, 'My comment is no doubt naive . . . ' are framing statements that
are clearly not meant to be taken at face value, since they carry (self-
protective) metamessages attesting to the intelligence or sophistication of a speaker who is able to discriminate the clever from the
stupid, the sophisticated from the naive. Naming the frame here
does indeed invoke something different. On the other hand a
response such as 'They're only playing' to the question 'What's
going on: are they fighting or only playing?' names the frame
without in any way changing it.

The source of possible confusion here would seem to stem from
the fact that, generally speaking, frames as metamessages are not
explicitly signalled to the interlocutor. This means that if a
metamessage is announced as such, it may well be reframed as
implying a meta-metamessage of the kind suggested above. Thus,
if one frames a talk with a statement like, 'I'd like to have a little chat
with you', a meta-metamessage of serious discussion may be

conveyed rather than the literal meaning. In a similar way, irony and sarcasm may be produced by framing an utterance in ways that serve to change the sign of the apparent message.

Framing and reframing: a dynamic process

Throughout her analyses, what Tannen stresses is the fact that negotiations of power are always involved in our conversational exchanges as we juggle conflicting needs for involvement and independence. For Tannen, frames are not static structures like the borders of a picture 'but are constantly evolving lines of interpretation, continually negotiated footings. The framing that is going on at any moment is part of what establishes the frame for what goes on next, and is partly created by the framing that went before' (ibid.:78).

In stressing the dynamic, interactive aspect of the process of interpretation, Tannen acknowledges the influence of Frederick Bartlett's early pioneering work on memory processes. For Bartlett, the past is stored in memory 'as an organized mass' rather than as 'a group of elements each of which retains its specific character' (1932:197). He uses the term 'schema' to refer to the organising principle at work in these memory structures. Remembering a text, in Bartlett's view, is therefore never a matter of accurate recall of detail, but rather a constructive process involving interaction between the text and the various schemata activated by the reading process. Reference to these experientially based clusters of knowledge may supply us with 'remembered' details never mentioned in the original text. What Bartlett stresses throughout is that schemata are not static entities, but 'active, developing patterns', constantly modified by our ongoing experience (ibid.:201).

What's in a frame?

Following Bartlett, Tannen uses the term 'frame' to refer not only to metamessages—those contextualising cues which guide our interpretation of utterances—but also to the structures of expectations (the 'extratextual' baggage) which we bring to the interpretive task. These can be thought of as experiential frames, or socio-cognitive points of reference which interact with the cues referred to above. Just as certain kinds of experience may make us attentive to particular aspects of a text, the ways in which texts are framed may equally seem to demand particular modes of reading. In 'What's in a Frame: Surface Evidence for Underlying Expectations' (1979), Tannen details the results of an experiment which set out to find linguistic evidence for the existence of frames and what they might contain.

As she points out, few researchers have investigated what frames or 'expectation structures' (she uses the terms interchangeably in this article) might consist of or how they may be culturally determined (ibid.:144). Indeed, cross-cultural differences are often the clearest indication of 'how we can know what's in a frame'. In an experiment carried out in ten different countries, subjects were shown a short silent film which they then had to describe to another person who, they were told, had not seen the film. The movie depicted among other things the theft of a basket of pears from a man picking the fruit by the side of a road. Tannen supervised the experiment in Greece and subsequently analysed the narratives produced. What she found was consistent with Bartlett's experiments in the 1930s: 'subjects organized and altered the actual contents of the movie in many ways' (ibid.:145) as they attempted to articulate what they had seen.

In the course of her analysis, Tannen isolated and examined several kinds of linguistic evidence which, she argued, revealed 'the imposition of the speakers' expectations on the content of the film' (ibid.). Such evidence included omissions, additions, inferences, repetitions, generalisations, incorrect statements and moral judgements. Moreover, when the American and Greek narratives were compared in terms of their recall of particular elements in the film, it appeared that expectations 'are often culturally determined, as one would expect' (ibid.). A noteworthy omission that would seem to support this view was the fact that, whereas all the American subjects mentioned that a man passes with a goat, three of the fourteen Greeks who referred to this man made no mention of the goat. As Tannen states:

> The conclusion suggested is that it is less remarkable, less unexpected, for Greeks that a passing man should be leading a

goat. In Schank and Abelson's terms, the goat is in the Greek's script for passing country person. For Americans, however, the goat is unexpected and therefore reportable. We may say that the Greeks omitted to mention the goat and thereby revealed something about their expectations. (ibid.:167)

The collected data revealed expectations not only about the objects and events shown in the film but also about the experimental situation itself, about watching a film, and about the act of retelling a story. As we noted in Chapter 2, watching a film involves much more than the passive reception of sound and image. The viewer's expectations and other framing devices associated with the film medium constantly mediate, as Tannen concludes in her article, 'between a person and her/his perceptions, and between those perceptions and the telling about them' (ibid.:166).

4

Knowledge Frames and Framing Knowledge

A new collaborative field

The mid-1970s, as Schank and Abelson (1977) point out, saw the emergence of a new field called 'cognitive science'. It was concerned with developing theories of knowledge systems, and it involved the collaboration of linguists, social psychologists and artificial intelligence (AI) researchers. (Schank himself has a background in AI, and Abelson is a social psychologist.) The climate for this cross-disciplinary convergence of interest in the nature of knowledge and the way it is used in understanding texts was created in part by major reorientations in the participating disciplines. Previously, psychologists had tended to neglect the study of unobservable mental processes, and had restricted stimulus material in their experiments on memory and learning to unconnected and artificial instances of language (1977:5–6). New experimental research in the 1960s and 1970s attempted to go beyond these limitations and to address the problem of how we understand and recall 'real-world' texts. At the same time, in the field of linguistics there was a move away from the analysis of exemplary sentences (isolated from any communicative context) to the analysis of naturally occurring texts. This involved acknowledging the role of socio-cultural as well as purely formal or grammatical knowledge in understanding texts (de Beaugrande, 1980:14; Fairclough, 1989:6–7). In addition, the renewed efforts of AI researchers to develop computer programs that could deal with natural language (as opposed to computer or logical languages) gave added impetus to the drive for more theoretically sophisticated models of how human understanding occurs.

The establishment of a new field concerned with cognitive processes encouraged an unprecedented number of collaborative interdisciplinary projects on the processing and comprehension of natural language texts. This in turn led to a proliferation of terminology, including the metaphor of the frame. As previously noted, Deborah Tannen (1979) provides a useful overview of the field, clarifying a potentially confusing array of different terms.

Top-down and bottom-up processing

The underlying assumption of researchers collaborating in this new field is that memory and perception are inextricably linked (Schank and Abelson, 1977:17). This view is consistent with a psychological tradition going back to Bartlett, who emphasised that what we think of as acts of perception are really acts of recall ([1932] 1972:14). Experiments such as Tannen's, referred to in the previous chapter, seem to support this approach since they have shown that only a small part of a visual scene is actually perceived by a viewer, the gaps being filled in (sometimes incorrectly) on the basis of expectations derived from previous experience (1979). The understanding of verbal texts is similarly 'expectation-driven' as readers supply details not explicitly stated. As Brown and Yule remark, 'one of the pervasive illusions which persists in the analysis of language is that we understand the meaning of a linguistic message solely on the basis of the words and structure of the sentence(s) used to convey that message' (1983:223).

In Chapter 1 we drew attention to the kinds of 'extratextual' knowledge involved in even the shortest of texts. Such knowledge includes recognition of genres or discourse types, as well as specific 'local' knowledge and socio-cultural or world knowledge of the broadest kind. For instance, to make sense of a simple statement like 'Black is beautiful' scrawled on a wall involves more than understanding the meaning of the individual words and their relationship to each other. To recognise this statement as a slogan from a certain period, making a political point about black pride, presupposes not only the ability to frame it as a complete text of a particular generic kind (i.e., as a slogan). It also presupposes access to certain kinds of socio-cultural knowledge (the marginalisation of blacks in North American society). Similarly a statement like 'We are all German Jews' (featured on banners carried by French students in May 1968) would be mystifying to anyone ignorant of the political circumstances of its utterance.

To use a distinction commonly made in the cognitive sciences, interpreting a text involves not only 'bottom-up' processing—building up a composite meaning on the basis of our perception of its component parts—but also 'top-down' processing on the basis of expectations, assumptions and prior knowledge brought to the text by the interpreter. Recent research in discourse analysis has shown, for instance, that assumptions about context influence the way in which the linguistic features of the text are processed (Fairclough, 1989:151). Tannen's investigation of the recall of visual images in a film draws similar conclusions about the role played by the experimental situation itself as the context for recounting the film (Tannen, 1979).

Inferences drawn in both bottom-up and top-down processing are based on knowledge derived from past experience of similar situations. As Schank and Abelson put it: 'Understanding is a process by which people match what they see and hear to pre-stored groupings of actions that they have already experienced' (1977:67). In the case of written texts, they stress that 'it is pragmatics—the way things usually work, not how they might conceivably work—which most often impels the reader towards an interpretation' (ibid.:9). Knowledge of the way things usually work implies the existence of the 'pre-stored groupings of actions' referred to above. 'Memory', they theorise, 'is organised around personal experiences or episodes rather than around abstract semantic categories' (ibid.:17–18). As the organising basis for this experiential knowledge, they postulate the existence of 'scripts', 'plans' and 'goals', structures that involve increasing levels of abstraction. They note that elsewhere these have been called 'frames' (Minsky, 1975) and 'schemata' (Bartlett, [1932] 1972; Rumelhart, 1975). The most intriguing question raised by such theories is how experience is organised and stored so that only a small part of it relevant to the interpretive task at hand gets activated at any given moment.

Frames for representing knowledge

Dieter Metzing, the editor of a collection of research papers entitled *Frame Conceptions and Text Understanding* (1980), points out that the book's exclusive focus is on 'interactions between text sentences on the one hand and a knowledge base on the other'. Analysing a text in terms of its specific 'structural and stylistic properties' is not, he adds, considered at all (ibid.:vii). Thus, although the interactive aspect of text–interpreter relations is recognised, only certain kinds of extratextual knowledge are relevant to the models proposed in his book. Metzing adds that 'future research' may change this emphasis since knowledge about text-types (genres) and stylistic and structural properties of texts could also 'be organized in terms of frames' (ibid.).

The lack of progress to this second stage has limited the usefulness of the cognitive approach to the understanding of texts outside the world of computer programming. Its explanatory value is further limited by a failure to consider how texts and the mediating contexts of their production and reception trigger particular frames. In the real world, as opposed to the world of artificial intelligence, the comprehension of texts does not occur in the socio-cultural vacuum of 'white-room' experimentation (Frake, 1980:49); nor is meaning-making a simple, one-way process.

The limitations of cognitive frame theory in relation to written texts are not at all surprising if one considers that the metaphor of the 'frame', first used by Marvin Minsky in 'A Framework for Representing Knowledge', developed in the context of making a robot that could see. Minsky's concern was thus with problems of visual knowledge and spatial orientation rather than with linguistic understanding (1975; condensed version reprinted in Metzing, 1980). What Minsky stresses in his influential paper is 'the expectation-driven aspects of recognition and comprehension', aspects which presuppose 'special devices' for organising and selecting relevant knowledge (Metzing, 1980:viii). These special devices he describes as frame-like structures stored in the memory, which organise past experience not as separate facts but in a topically or sequentially interlinked fashion: 'When one encounters a new situation (or makes a substantial change in one's view of a problem), one selects from memory a structure called a frame. This is a remembered framework to be adapted to fit reality by changing details as necessary' (Minsky, 1980:1).

Minsky's frames (like 'scripts' and 'schemata') are organised bundles of related world-knowledge: they represent our generalised experiences of stereotypical activities, conventional processes, syntactic and other linguistic structures, arrangements of objects in space, and so on. Attached to these frames are different kinds of information. 'Some of this information is about how to use the frame. Some is about what one can expect to happen next. Some is about what to do if these expectations are not confirmed' (ibid.). The question that Minsky elides is how, of all the available frame systems, a particular one gets activated in the first place. As he puts it, a frame system 'is evoked when evidence and expectation make it plausible that the scene in view will fit it' (ibid.:5). What would constitute 'evidence', and how expectations come to be triggered prior to the selection of a particular frame, are details left unspecified by Minsky. Since his emphasis is on robotic orientation in space, the ways in which a verbal text might 'cue' the interpreter to apply a particular frame remain outside the scope of his discussion.

Minsky's frames are networks of 'nodes and relations'. The top levels are those fixed, invariable aspects of a given situation, while the bottom levels have many 'slots' or terminals into which optional elements may be fitted. Normally these are already filled with 'default assignments'. For example, if a 'cinema-going frame' is activated in a text, it can be assumed by default that watching a film presupposes buying a ticket and taking one's seat; such details do not have to be specifically mentioned by the writer. Readers constantly and automatically supply default elements of this kind whenever they read. Furthermore, since individual frame-systems are 'linked by an information retrieval network', a replacement frame can be activated if the chosen frame does not fit reality. As Minsky concludes, 'These interframe structures make possible other ways to represent knowledge about facts, analogies, and other information useful in understanding' (ibid.:2).

Frame semantics or checklist theories?

The alternative representations Minsky presumably has in mind would include so-called 'checklist' descriptions of meaning. Researchers in semantic theory who subscribe to this view 'regard the meaning of a linguistic form as best expressed in terms of an exhaustive checklist of the conditions that must be satisfied in order for one to be able to say that the word had been appropriately used' (Fillmore, 1977:68). This involves examining boundaries of the application of particular words. For example, boundary research on words like 'widow' and 'bachelor' would generate the following kinds of questions (ibid.:70):

> Is it correct to say that Pope John XXIII died a bachelor?
> Would you call a woman a widow who murdered her husband?

On the other hand, theories like Minsky's, based on an appeal to 'prototypes', take a much simpler approach to the problem of meaning. In this view, no elaborate logical analysis is required: novel situations or particular lexical items are automatically matched with a prototype or prototypical situation stored in the memory and accepted as sufficiently similar or dissimilar. As Fillmore notes, 'the process of using a word in a novel situation involves comparing current experiences with past experiences and judging whether they are similar enough to call for the same linguistic encoding' (ibid.:57). Despite the obvious theoretical alignment with cognitive frame theories, Fillmore's notion of a 'frame semantics' is potentially confusing. A 'frame' in his usage refers to 'the system of linguistic choices . . . that can get associated with prototypical instances of scenes' (Fillmore, 1975:124). In other words, 'frames' are the lexical choices which activate standard or prototypical 'scenes' or contexts, and vice versa.

Meaning acquisition, according to Fillmore, seems to provide evidence of the usefulness of this approach, since our knowledge of linguistic forms first comes to us through association with personally meaningful contexts or particular 'scenes'. The meaning of the word 'pencil' may thus be built up on the basis of experiences connected with the 'scene' of drawing. This scene comes to be associated with certain linguistic 'frames', of which 'pencil' is only one instance. Scenes will thus trigger associated frames (or linguistic choices) and vice versa. Such a scene-and-frame analysis (reminiscent of Minsky's frame levels) sheds light, Fillmore contends, on the processes of recall and comprehension. For particular linguistic choices in a text will activate certain scenes for the interpreter, on the basis of which s/he will fill in gaps and make connections with other larger scenes. These activities are based 'not on information that gets explicitly coded in the linguistic signal, but on what the interpreter knows about the larger scenes that this material activates or creates' (ibid.:75). How this actually occurs is not specified by Fillmore. Scene-and-frame analysis is also useful, he further notes, in elucidating problems of translation from one language to another. For instance, an analysis of two words that appear to be acceptable translations of each other will often reveal important differences in the kinds of scenes they evoke. 'Téléphone', for instance, may well call up a café scene for a French speaker, whereas 'telephone' is unlikely to have such an association for an English speaker.

Problems in synonymy can also be addressed within this framework. Two different linguistic frames (to use Fillmore's example, 'weewee' and 'urinate') can be said to evoke the same cognitive scene, but the interactional scenes are (presumably) quite different. Thus one advantage of Fillmore's scene-and-frame couplet is that its hyphenated character draws attention to the link between language and the contexts of its use. Both 'scene' and 'frame' are necessary terms, insists Fillmore, since sometimes one of the pair remains stable while the other may change. He gives as an example the situation where learning what to call a familiar but previously nameless object (like a traffic chicane) causes a change of frame without involving any change of scene.

In conclusion, Fillmore acknowledges that although frame semantics may provide a useful conceptual framework for dealing with a number of sub-fields in the study of meaning and comprehension, his research is no more than a 'tentative first step in seeking a solution to certain problems in semantic theory within the framework of concepts that seems to be emerging in a number of disciplines touching on human thought and behaviour' (ibid.:79).

Cognitive frames and framing

Frame conceptions of understanding imply acts of framing rather than the passive decoding of linguistic signs: 'understanding is a process by which people match what they see and hear to pre-stored groupings of actions that they have already experienced' (Schank and Abelson, 1977:67). Nevertheless, both Minsky and his followers tend to focus on *frames* as storage systems rather than on *framing* as a dynamic activity. Charniak is quite explicit about this: 'I take a frame to be a static data structure about one stereotyped topic' (1975:42, cited in Tannen, 1979:139). Schank and Abelson prefer the more theatrical metaphor of 'scripts' since it emphasises both the sequential or episodic aspect of particular kinds of experience and the role-oriented bias operating in perception. Yet they similarly stress the relatively stable, predetermined nature of these theoretical entities: 'A script is a structure that describes appropriate sequences of events in a particular context. A script is made up of slots and requirements about what can fill those slots . . . A script is a predetermined, stereotyped sequence of actions that defines a well-known situation' (1977:41).

As such definitions reveal, cognitive frame conceptions shed little light on the problem of change—how new experiences interact with and modify existing frames, and how changes in frames affect interpretation. Several questions remain unanswered, and many are simply not addressed. How much information is stored in frames and how are they interconnected? How do we acquire frames in the first place? What roles do factors like gender and socio-cultural or racial difference play in their determination and significance? How are they shaped by ideology? Which particular frames get selected in an act of interpretation? On what basis? How do we decide whether a frame is appropriate? Do frames model the way all knowledge is organised or only certain kinds of experiential knowledge? As Metzing concedes, frames are no more than 'working concepts' that have proved 'useful for some time in attempts to develop a new theory of human information processing . . . and as such they may soon be replaced by other "working concepts"' (1980:xi).

In fact it could be argued that the 'script' metaphor works better than the 'frame' metaphor as a way of representing certain types of knowledge, particularly the procedural or sequential kind. As used by cognitive scientists, neither metaphor sheds much light on the complexities of interpreting texts outside the laboratory. Given their emphasis on computer programming, AI researchers are bound to regard issues like cognitive frame content and specification as more relevant to their research than the broader societal and institutional frameworks within which meanings are normally negotiated. Furthermore, in view of the complexities of programming involved, neither circumtextual nor intertextual frames—both of which play a significant role in directing and constraining interpretation—have yet been taken into account.

For similar reasons, intratextual framing possibilities have also been ignored. These relate to both the spatial and temporal aspects of the reading process. For instance, since reading is an activity that takes place in time, the point that we have reached in a given text at a particular moment affects how we interpret the information offered to us at that stage. New information causes us to reframe what has gone before and affects our expectations of what lies ahead. (Similarly, deviating from the prescribed order of reading will affect how we interpret what we read.) Since reading is also an activity with spatial dimensions, other factors which affect interpretation include how words are represented typographically on the page, as well as where texts are located physically in space (scrawled on a wall, inscribed in stone, or printed on a badge). Recognition of intratextual and other framing devices at work in the understanding of texts may well depend on the activation of extratextual knowledge organised in frame-like structures in the memory. Unfortunately the models offered so far by the cognitive sciences do little to elucidate the complexities of this process. A comprehensive account of interpretation in framing terms would need to engage with the semiotically oriented frame theories, as well as with the classificatory data-structures postulated by cognitive and social scientists.

It must be remembered that AI researchers are a long way from claiming to have solved the problem of how we make sense of texts. The issues they raise are those most relevant to the programming of computers for very specific tasks, and their research projects are necessarily extremely limited in aim and scope. Typical is Charniak's computer program called 'Ms Malaprop', whose function is to answer simple questions about simple stories dealing with the mundane activity of painting furniture (1979).

Framing educational knowledge: Basil Bernstein

Before Minsky raised the curtain on cognitive science with his innovative 1975 article on general knowledge-frames, and before Goffman gave a new direction to social psychology with his 1974 book *Frame Analysis*, Basil Bernstein had already introduced the concept of framing, somewhat idiosyncratically, into his sociological studies of educational knowledge. Bernstein's influential essay 'On the Classification and Framing of Educational Knowledge' (1971) is based on the idea, drawn partly from the anthropologist Mary Douglas, that our ways of interpreting and ordering experience have much to do with the variable strength of certain 'boundary' relationships.

In her structuralist study of symbolic cultural pollution, *Purity and Danger*, Douglas broaches several of the themes taken up by later writers on framing, and indeed uses the terms 'frame' and 'framing function' in her account of ritual mechanisms used to 'limit experience, shut in desired themes or shut out intruding ones' ([1966] 1978:63). Her demonstration that 'any structure of ideas is vulnerable at its margins' (ibid.:121)—an insight subsequently extended by Goffman—is seen by Bernstein as having particular relevance to the formal organisation of knowledge through educational systems and institutions. He acknowledges ([1971] 1975:227) that his 'greatest debt' is to the work of Douglas.

Though interested primarily in issues of curriculum and pedagogy, Bernstein views framing in a manner that has close affinity with the approach taken by cognitive scientists. Like them, he is more concerned with 'message systems' (ibid.:203) than metamessages, and with general coded structures rather than individual acts of encoding or structuration. Cognitive science in the mid-1970s tended to focus on data-structures pertaining to conventional sets of arrangements such as the layout of a certain kind of room, and Bernstein himself chooses that very example for an exposition of 'classification and framing'. He asks us to imagine the typical furnishings of two different kinds of (English) middle-class living-rooms: one late Victorian, the other in a trendy modern suburb like Hampstead. The Victorian room is likely to contain many objects, the other relatively few: 'in one case the object array is foreground and the space background, whereas in the second case the space is a vital component of the array' (ibid.:232). But in both, he says, the array of objects is 'strongly classified': that is, the tacit rules controlling their choice and arrangment are firm for each kind of room. The Victorian room also exhibits 'strong framing', in the sense that the distinctive structure of its object array would remain constant over a long period. In the Hampstead room, on the other hand, 'the objects are likely to enter into a variety of relationships with each other; this would indicate weak framing' (ibid.).

Classification, then, has to do with rules of exclusion, while framing has to do with the extent to which objects in the array can be differently combined. Before considering how Bernstein applies these concepts to educational settings, it is useful to note how he proceeds to elaborate on the issue of control, because this is where he parts company with the cognitive scientists. In this more developed (and thoroughly British) example, he describes four kinds of domestic lavatory, ranging from one that is strongly classified (bare walls, gleaming white washbowl, tidily placed soap and towel, covered paper dispenser) to one that is weakly classified (decorated walls, an untidy variety of reading matter, uncovered toilet roll). The first is a space regulated by strong rules of exclusion, in that it is sharply demarcated from other spaces in the house. It is also strongly framed, in that communication between occupants of the space and those outside the locked door is minimal. Accordingly, Bernstein remarks, 'there must be strong boundary maintainers (authority) . . . to ensure the apartness of things' (ibid.:233). And yet there is an irony in this, because 'providing that the classification and framing is not violated, the user of the space is beyond surveillance' (ibid.:235). In contrast, the fourth lavatory, which seems at first to be a very relaxed space, conveys the tacitly constraining message that occupants are expected *not* to set themselves apart, not to lock the door (if there is one), not to tidy up the apparent disorder, not to avoid conversation with anyone nearby, not to subdue somatic sound effects, not to prevent the pet cat from entering the occupied space, and so forth. Therefore, 'in as much as the framing between inside and outside is weak then it is also the case that the user is potentially or indirectly under continuous surveillance, in which case there is no privacy' (ibid.).

With this homely analogy, Bernstein tries to illuminate the subtle potency of 'boundary maintenance' as it occurs in those formal structures, codes and processes which institutionalise the acquisition of knowledge.

Power at the margins

Educational knowledge, a 'major regulator of the structure of experience' (ibid.:202), is realised through three 'message systems': curriculum (what counts as valid knowledge), pedagogy (what counts as valid transmission of knowledge), and evaluation (what counts as valid demonstration that the knowledge has been acquired). Each of these message systems rests on the concepts of classification and framing, which relate to one another in a distinctive way within any particular society, because their strength can vary independently. With regard to curricular structures, classification 'refers to the degree of boundary maintenance between contents' (ibid.:205). For instance, if school x assumes that Chemistry is Chemistry and Biology is Biology and never the twain shall meet, this strongly classified (compartmentalised) relation will determine many procedures, ranging from the school's subject timetables to its way of assessing student performance. Framing, on the other hand, 'refers to the degree of control teacher and pupil possess over the selection, organisation, and pacing of the knowledge transmitted and received in the pedagogical relationship' (ibid.:205–6). A learning process is strongly framed if the teacher exerts tight control over the rate at which a class is permitted to learn.

One problem with Bernstein's notion of framing is that it turns out to be hardly separable from his notion of classification. He broadens his definition of framing, for instance, by applying it not only to the respective roles of teacher and student in controlling what may be taught but also to the relationship between educational knowledge and everyday knowledge acquired outside school. How this boundary differs in principle from the kind that separates curriculum *a* from curriculum *b* is not clear. In other words, Bernstein regards frames as classificatory in effect; his emphasis is virtually structuralist in tendency.

Nevertheless his interest in power relationships distinguishes Bernstein clearly from the cognitive scientists, because he recognises that boundaries imply strategies of boundary maintenance, and that these imply hierarchical social structures. Declaring that 'power relationships are expressed through boundary relationships' (ibid.:17), he sets out a typology of educational knowledge codes, based on two broad kinds of curricula: a 'collection code', featuring strong classification, and an 'integrated code', featuring weak classification. The framing of each can vary. In European education, where there is usually an explicit syllabus with few options available to teacher or student, the collection code tends to be strongly classified and strongly framed. In North America, on the other hand, where a greater range of subject combinations is possible and there is little insulation between academic and everyday knowledge, both classification and framing tend to be weaker than in other instances of the collection code: they are thus closer to the integrated code, which by definition is weakly classified though its framing is variable. What distinguishes an integrated code is that it involves 'the *subordination* of previously insulated subjects or courses to some *relational* idea, which blurs the boundaries between the subjects' (ibid.:209). Thus a university course on the English novel may include a couple of French works in translation, a non-fictional work, and some Marxist theory, while yet remaining within the principles of a collection code; whereas by contrast a course on Myth, which subordinates questions about national or generic categories and selects diverse texts on the basis of mythological themes, belongs to an integrated code.

Disciplinary frames

In European traditions of formal knowledge, adherence to what Bernstein has called a collection code is evident in the strictness of the disciplinary practices that separate one subject from another and train students to confine themselves to a hierarchical ethos:

> The key concept of the European collection code is discipline. This means learning to work *within* a received frame. It means, in particular, *learning* what questions can be put at any particular time. Because of the hierarchical ordering of knowledge in *time*, certain questions raised may not enter into a particular frame.
>
> This is soon learned by both teachers and pupils. Discipline then means accepting a given selection, organisation, pacing and timing of knowledge realized in the pedagogical frame . . . In a sense, the European form of the collection code makes knowledge safe through the process of socialization into its frames. There is a tendency, which varies with the strength of specific frames, for the young to be socialized into assigned principles and routine operations and derivations. The evaluative system places an emphasis upon attaining *states* of knowledge rather than *ways* of knowing. (ibid.:214)

On the other hand, the greater openness of learning under an integrated code can exert power over the student by a different method. As with the 'weakly framed lavatory' example cited above, a weakly framed pedagogic situation makes public a greater range of the student's behaviour. Thoughts and values thus become more available for control, and socialisation into the code 'could be more intensive and perhaps more penetrating' (ibid.:224).

Generalising from Bernstein's remarks about the concept of an academic discipline, one could say that different disciplinary conventions amount largely to certain habits of 'extratextual' framing. Thus the methods adopted by historians in interpreting phenomena will depend on sets of assumptions, interests and investments; accordingly a historian will tend to approach written documents with different questions in mind from those that seem proper to a literary critic or an anthropologist. These extratextually framed differences remain significant even when exponents of the separate disciplines make occasional use of shared methodologies.

Disciplinary frames can therefore pose a problem for scholars who try to work outside them. A case in point is the mixed reception given to an interdisciplinary book by Bob Hodge and Vijay Mishra, *Dark Side of the Dream: Australian Literature and the Postcolonial*

Mind (1991). Some reviewers judged it in terms of historiographic etiquette, some in terms of anthropological etiquette, and so on. Ensuing correspondence in the columns of newspapers and journals concentrated on debates about the relevance of these respective frameworks. Some thought anthropology should provide the norms of reference for such a study; others thought the new interdisciplinary field of cultural studies had discredited anthropology as a framer of incorrigibly bad habits. History was also invoked in the cause of boundary maintenance: one reviewer declared that 'this book contains a number of empirical errors of a type that historians . . . simply do not make' (Wolfe, 1992: 334). Hodge and Mishra retorted: 'the historian's reading method produces an "empirical error", which the historian then exposes and castigates, while we semioticians look on in awe and amazement at our irrelevance to the whole performance' (Hodge and Mishra, 1992: 878). Their main defence, however, is that 'this whole opposition is misconceived':

> A good case can be made that semiotics and history have complementary blind spots in their reading strategies: semioticians tend to get too much from reading too few texts, where historians get too little from reading too many. Ways of reading are not mere techniques that can be easily learnt or unlearnt. They are bound up with the ideology of a discipline, part of the construction of an individual identity as historian or semiotician. But the boundaries around two adjacent areas such as history and semiotics can be transgressed, as many interdisciplinary forays have shown, without jeopardising the integrity and permanence of the two established disciplines. (ibid.:880)

Yet more is involved than just making interdisciplinary forays. Once the boundaries that demarcate a field of knowledge are called into question, more specific issues soon arise about its constituent assumptions. In *The Gendered Framing of English Teaching* (1991), Diana Kelly-Byrne records the findings of her ethnographic study of gender orderings in a coeducational school community, particularly in the means by which English is taught there. She investigates how 'students learn to adduce frames of reference so that they can make sense of the texts they encounter', 'what procedures, classificatory acts and "sets" are used' by the teachers, and whether 'these acts of framing carry a gender bias' or in other ways encourage students 'to read or interpret texts in unduly restrictive ways' (Kelly-Byrne, 1991:4). She finds that in many respects the English classroom fosters framing practices which 'support and elaborate a patriarchal narrative' (ibid.:104).

Sinclair and Coulthard (1975) have studied the language of classroom interactions at the micro-discursive level, noting that teachers typically control the structure of lessons by using certain linguistic 'frames' in ways that would be inappropriate in an ordinary conversational transaction. Seemingly casual utterances such as 'Well, I thought we'd do three quizzes today' are devices of control, and reflect hierarchical power relationships. If anyone were to begin a conversation with friends at a dinner table by saying 'Well, I thought we'd spend this evening with a discussion of my recent holiday', the gambit would be taken ironically. In the terms used by Sinclair and Coulthard, this element of classroom discourse, which signals the beginning or end of what the teacher regards as a stage in the lesson, is called a 'boundary exchange', and is seen as comprising the functions of 'framing' and 'focusing' (ibid.:22, 49).

Reframing texts in the classroom

Kelly-Byrne's questions about whether students are taught to read and interpret texts in unduly restrictive ways, and whether there is room for alternative approaches, have been posed in other discussions of the framing of texts in the classroom. MacLachlan (1988) argues against the view that teaching situations homogenise irresistibly anything read in class and flatten out generic distinctions. She contends that the typical framing effect of the pedagogic occasion itself tends to activate other framing operations. Accordingly an institutional set-up such as an English lesson, for which the reading conventions of literary analysis are requisite, focuses a student's mind in a particularly conscious way on those other framing features (intertextuality, for instance), which—ironically—are resistant to mere assimilation within the broad genre of 'the set text'. Reid (1990) argues that although student readers have routinely learnt to regard a text as self-bounded and equipped with fixed reference points for interpretation, these limits which the traditional English course imposes on reading practices can readily be modified by strategies of reframing. He describes a classroom experiment based on three versions of a particular text: two videotapes which used different camera angles to record simultaneously the 'same' performance, and also the script for that performance. One aim in bringing these different versions together was to discover whether students find it easy to recognise that any interpretation is framed, and may be reframed—sometimes in quite material ways.

The primary text used in this experiment was a short piece of minimally punctuated prose by Ania Walwicz, a writer and performance artist. As initially presented to the student readers (stripped of such circumtextual elements as authorial name and title, and lacking any explanatory preamble), it raised questions about the means by which one tries to derive significance from a text when it is apparently devoid of the usual overt 'frame-setting' messages. Subsequently the two screen versions were presented for comparison with each other and with the printed version. Therefore the text (or cluster of texts) signalled its substance *as text*: the students could no longer interpret it as a mere slice of 'unmediated' experience, and their attention was drawn to several features of 'literary' reading practices.

The next chapter will take up the general issue of specifying how one recognises various frame-setting messages and generic cues to interpretation in the reading of written texts.

5

Generic Framings of Written Texts

Insurance against risk

No communication can take place without interpretation, and no interpretation can take place without framing. But written texts are framed in especially complex ways. To communicate in writing is to run a greater risk of being misunderstood than in face-to-face conversation, where the intended sense of words can be checked against their immediate circumstances ('Lovely day!', you say—yet the rain is pelting down) and against accompanying gestures (a beaming smile, a wink, a raised eyebrow, a smirk, a scowl). Written texts, detached by the very nature of their medium from an initial act of inscription, usually take out insurance against that risk: they rely on emphatic or intricate framing devices in an effort to curtail the reader's interpretive licence. Some of these devices may be attributable to authorial cunning, some to editorial or other media-tion. In turn, the reader will bring various interests and notions to bear on the text, thus framing it extratextually in ways which may or may not be attentive to what the text supplies. Meanings are generated at the point where various frames meet. Any particular interpretation is the outcome of a struggle (frequently unacknowl-edged, even unconscious) for semantic control, as different framings compete with one another.

How one answers such basic questions as 'Is this a literary work?' and 'What exactly is its genre?' will depend on which frames are dominating one's reception of the text. Even minimal written forms such as graffiti, slogans or epitaphs cannot be comprehended unless they are framed in some way. Their words alone can never indicate reliably how they should be used and interpreted. In order to decide what kind of text is being read, readers always need to 'place' it in relation to comparable texts, in relation to surrounding information, and so on. To read generically is to posit frames for interpreting the language used.

The case of epitaphs

Some problematic aspects of genre and framing have been examined by Reid (1988a) in relation to one exemplary 'set' of minimal texts, namely epitaphs. The following discussion draws extensively on Reid's article, which poses a seemingly simple question: How can anyone identify particular texts as belonging to an epitaphic set? According to certain linguists, it should be possible to specify an amalgam of lexical and grammatical features that distinguish epitaphs clearly and reliably. 'Obligatory elements define the genre to which a text belongs', insist Halliday and Hasan (1985:61). Yet to inspect a large sample of the texts that we readily recognise as epitaphs is to discover no such invariable constraints applying to them. At that level of linguistic analysis they just do not bear any collective distinguishing marks.

This point would not have surprised the eighteenth-century lexicographer and literary wit, Samuel Johnson. 'To define an Epitaph is useless', he remarked tersely. 'Everyone knows that it is an inscription on a tomb. An Epitaph, therefore, implies no particular character of writing . . . [and] has no rule to restrain or mollify it, except this, that it ought not to be longer than common beholders may have leisure or patience to peruse' (quoted in Owen and Smyser, 1974:49).

Johnson's brusque truism does not close the subject, of course. If an epitaph is simply the type of text that gets engraved over graves, and if genre is thus a locative phenomenon rather than a purely linguistic one, the implications are best understood in terms of framing. Take the words *'Tis I; be not afraid.* What do they signify? Nothing definite, until a reader associates them with a genre—that is, with some type of textual situation and with some system of signs. And to identify the genre, more information is necessary. This point may not seem obvious, because certainly the group of words does have intrinsic linguistic features that indicate limits on the ways in which it *could* be used (for instance, this is not the way people speak in ordinary conversation today). But the words alone do not tell us how they *are* being used, and only that can specify their significance. The utterance needs to be placed; there must be a framed occasion, for every genre depends on a conventional set of ways of indicating a location, a semiotic space within which particular objects (texts) can be made to mean something.

How then would we interpret such a statement when incised on a particular tombstone? (It used to be a popular choice for that purpose.) As an epitaph, the text acquires at once a measure of significance in relation to the space that it delineates. It probably accompanies the name and death-date of a deceased person; it is set into a carved stone, surrounded by other such stones; there are memorial tokens on all sides. It thus marks a liminal space where the body has been separated from bereaved associates and deposited in the ground. In recognising that placement, we are now framing the epitaphic text *circumtextually*. Its situation not only constitutes the physical borders (in this case, at the gravestone's edge) without which no text can seem to cohere, it also provides through adjacent signs (those of a cemetery, a church graveyard, or other such setting) a relevant semantic field of coherence—one that signifies mourning and consolation. This circumtextual framing can guide us to interpret the group of words as evoking the fear commonly associated with death only to dismiss it (be not afraid) because some speaker is reassuringly identified ('Tis I).

But at that point in the interpretive process another kind of framing, less tangible, must be adduced, because no aspect of the immediate material surroundings of the text can tell us directly how to construe this particular 'I'. Is a bereaved speaker supposedly addressing the deceased? Is the deceased supposedly addressing the bereaved, and by extension the passer-by? Neither interpretation would in itself explain the submerged link between each clause; why should the declaration of identity ('It is I') lend any authority to the command ('Be not afraid')? For an answer, one has to recognise that the text is also seeking to be framed *intertextually.* It is in fact a quoted phrase drawn from the gospel account of a miraculous appearance of Jesus to his disciples when he walked on water and calmed the storm. Therefore it has the borrowed status of a supposedly divine utterance, and in its application to the gravestone it can be imagined as spoken with supernatural authority to the deceased, to the bereaved, and to the passer-by.

In such cases a prior text is not just a source of allusions; rather, it provides materials for generic reframings. In other words, intertextuality refers to 'the passage from one sign system to another' (Kristeva, 1986:111): from ancient biblical scriptures or later evangelical hymns, for instance, to gravestone inscriptions. (For further examples, see Reid, 1988b:106–7.)

Other framing operations are applicable as well. The statement *Deeds are better things than words are, actions mightier than boastings,* when inscribed among a composite array of epitaphs on an imposingly expensive and expansive monument, invites a reader to interpret it as a comment on its own generic situation. To look at the text in this way is to frame it *intratextually.* For this to be applicable, a tombstone text must seem to comprise separate segments. There may be a narrative part that is fairly distinct from a more reflective part; there may be different inscriptions for different people buried at the same spot; there may be an intricate interplay of elements within a sculpted and multi-textual assemblage. Usually, however, the brevity of an epitaph gives no great scope for intratextual framing.

Yet there can be no interpretation without an interpreter. In order to activate the potential meanings of those intratextual, intertextual and circumtextual elements, a reader must frame them *extratextually,* drawing attitudes and aptitudes into the communicative exchange. *A lonesome man. In memory of all Jews destroyed in Europe*: coming across this inscription in an Australian cemetery, one can recognise the kind of story to which it alludes only to the extent that one frames it extratextually with appropriate information—by bringing to bear (having noted also the man's dates of birth and death) some awareness of the Holocaust and the plight of refugees.

Extratextual framing involves, then, something of what cognitive scientists refer to when they designate a body of knowledge that readers apply in processing texts. However, the concept of 'knowledge' commonly used in that field of research is open to criticism, as we noted in Chapter 4. Verdaasdonk (1982:87) remarks that 'cognitive psychology is curiously insensitive to the fact that what in a given domain counts as knowledge is always institutionally determined'. The relevant institutions include various social, cultural and educational establishments, each promoting or reinforcing a particular set of frames. Reading and writing practices are developed in and constrained by these. In the case of epitaphic texts, as we have noted, certain constructions of religious knowledge may shape the available meanings. What counts as appropriate for the purposes of extratextual framing will be constrained by other elements: circumtextual framing (for example a tombstone's site, size and style, all of which take institutionalised forms according to the practices and precepts of different religious denominations); intertextual framing (for example through scriptural and hymnic language, conventionally interpreted within particular church-governed habits of reading); and intratextual framing (for example a stone inscribed with both English and Hebrew characters, producing an internally disrupted text which comments wryly on its own piety: *Epitaphs on tombstones are trifles vainly spent; a man's good name is his best monument*).

Nevertheless, to a greater extent than most other genres, epitaphs tend to be distinguished most clearly by their location. As writing, they are removed in time from the moment of utterance; but as memorial markers, they are not normally removed in place from what they mark. Belonging on a gravestone, an epitaph functions as part of a signpost, announcing to the cemetery visitor: 'Here are the bones (or ashes) of x'. Therefore the very same words that commemorate the dead person on that spot have another function if transcribed to a page. Indeed, when an epitaph appears in a book it is generically different. 'Epitaph on Elizabeth, L. H.', a poem by Ben Jonson, implies in its title that it is *not* what it says it is, precisely because no gravestone text ever labels itself with the term 'epitaph'. This exemplifies the dictum that 'naming the frame invokes a different one' (Tannen, 1992:65). For despite the fact that they include phrases like 'in this vault', Jonson's lines are materially detached from their mortal referent—if they ever had one (Reid, 1989:205). Their genre is literary: the effects they produce are those of a poem.

The case of poetry

The contrast between an epitaph and a poem should not, however, be drawn too sharply. Much more than prose genres can, poetry does share with epitaphic texts a strong locative quality. On the page, a poem is immediately recognisable as such even before we read a word of it, because the conventions of its spatial arrangement proclaim its generic status. While typographical details may vary, the definitive line breaks with their surrounding blank areas will make it clear what type of text we are looking at: they demand that we read it as a poem.

Jonathan Culler demonstrates the framing power of these 'margins of silence' by chopping into short lines an item from a French newspaper. 'The words remain the same', he notes, 'but their effects for readers are substantially altered'. The new layout tells us 'how the sequence is to be read and what kind of interpretations may be derived from it' (1975:161). It is true that certain other aspects of a text also tend to be regarded as 'poetic', like heightened diction or regular rhythm; but in practice these are generically redundant. Some theorists have thought otherwise. Indeed the first literary critic to comment on the importance of frame effects, Barbara Herrnstein Smith in her 1968 book *Poetic Closure*, does suggest that it is intrinsic textual features alone that constitute a genre.

Smith posits a formal distinction between verse and prose by drawing comparisons with a passage of music, which 'frames itself, so to speak, by being more highly organised than anything else in the environment of sound or silence', and with a painting, which is 'framed not so much by the piece of wood around its borders as by the borders implied by its own internal structure'. In much the same way, Smith avers, a poem achieves coherence through meter, which serves 'as a frame for the poem, separating it from a "ground" of less highly structured speech and sound' (1968:23–4).

While this formalist observation is no doubt valid as far as it goes, it leaves out of account the increasing body of contemporary poetry that is not metrically structured. It also fails to explain how Culler's rearranged piece of prose comes to be read as a poem. Evidently, more is involved than just the recognition of metrical and other intratextual frames when a reader identifies a text as 'poetic'. Smith does not investigate this issue of the reader's role, which is given paramount emphasis by Stanley Fish in his anti-formalist response to the larger question: What is literature? Fish defines literature as 'language around which we have drawn a frame, a frame that indicates a decision to regard with a particular self-consciousness the resources language has always possessed . . . What characterises literature then are not formal properties, but an attitude—towards properties that belong by constitutive right to language' (1980:108–9). 'We', in Fish's formulation, refers to the 'community' of those who share certain strategies of interpretation, the community that exists at the point where texts and readers come together (ibid.:14).

As Fish implies, the trouble with purely formalist definitions of genre, like Smith's, is that they cannot explain how a pair of texts (or any other phenomena) whose formal properties are identical can come to be interpreted as generically different. Goffman's 'keyed' situations, Duchamp's bicycle wheel, the same paragraph moved from a cookbook into a novel—all show that genre, in a broad or narrow sense, is an effect of framing. And yet no one engaged in interpretation has total licence in this regard. Generic placement will depend not only on the framing impulses of interpreters but also on promptings by the text and the text's situation. These promptings may take the form of a distinctive typographic pattern of words on a page, a line drawn around an exhibit in a gallery, the relocation of an object in a new space that gives it a different semiotic charge, and so on.

Much of Smith's book concentrates on framing devices that seem to confer 'completeness' on particular poems. For instance poetry cast in stanza form lends itself to a simple kind of conclusive patterning; at the end of two of Wyatt's songs,

> the return to the opening stanza serves as a frame for what might be considered the 'song proper'. The framing stanzas announce that a song will be sung and then that it has just been sung. The advantage here is clear: the song itself need possess only the frailest thematic structure; closure is insured. (Smith, 1968:64)

Narrative lyrics permit a different framing effect: 'closure may be secured through the speaker's concluding turn or framing comment' (ibid.:126), as in Keats's 'Nightingale' ode, which ends with an ambiguous awakening from a trance. Smith also analyses more complicated framings in poems by Milton, Sidney and others. But no considered theory of framing emerges.

The case of literary prose

Anne Freadman observes that 'the publishing conventions that make books the way they are—with covers, titles, bibliographical and cataloguing information, title pages, tables of contents, acknowledgements, prefaces by series editors, footnotes, indices, glossaries, etc.—are notational frames for the ceremonies of reading . . . [and] have a great deal to do with the business of setting the genre of the text they enclose' (1987:114). Materials affixed or adjacent to a text can be especially important if it is written in prose, as most print texts are. A reader would often have difficulty in recognising the appropriate generic features of a prose text in the absence of an explicit initial orientation. Usually this is available through circumtextual guideposts such as those itemised by Freadman. Because prose is the 'ordinary' straightforward form of written discourse, relatively unmarked by salient typographical features and covering a wide range of possible text types, prose works will usually supply plenty of cues at the start so that a reader can see which particular kind of prose it aspires to be. Sometimes, however, the cues provided may contradict each other or seem to offer more than one framing possibility. Marguerite Duras subtitles a number of her fictional works 'texte-film-roman', evoking in the process a hybrid genre. Roland Barthes' *Barthes par lui-même* (Barthes by himself), seemingly defined as a particular type of text by its inclusion in an autobiographical series, similarly merges different genres by providing this comment on the inside front cover: 'Tout ceci doit être considéré comme dit par un personnage de roman' ('All this should be regarded as if spoken by a novelistic character').

In directing our perception of genre, circumtextual frames normally imply a particular contractual undertaking. This can be quite explicit, as in the case of formula fiction, where the standardised packaging—prominent authorial signature and series imprint, uniformity of cover design, and so on—signals in advance the novel's conformity to a genre, its offer of a story which is the same yet different (MacLachlan, 1993). The circumtext can also serve as a kind of advertising space, exploited for its seductive potential in targeting a particular readership. But there are other functions as well. Being a liminal or threshold phenomenon, the circumtext mediates our passage from everyday reality to the highly organised space of a fictional world. As Claude Duchet remarks, this transitional space is 'an indeterminate zone . . . where there are mixed two series of codes: the social code, in its advertising aspect, and the codes which complete or regulate the text' (quoted by Genette, 1991:271). It can thus become the location for metamessages that aim to exert control over what is enclosed. As Pearson remarks, the frame is the site 'where struggles for authority must inevitably be enacted' (1990:19). Like the nineteenth-century painters mentioned in Chapter 2, who reclaimed extra-compositional space in order to assert the authority of their particular artistic or social vision, prose-writers have often used preliminary statements for the purpose of directing their readers. Pearson gives detailed examples: Miguel de Cervantes' claim of authenticity in the preface to Part 2 of *Don Quixote*, Nathaniel Hawthorne's claim of historical accuracy through his 'Custom-House' sketch in *The Scarlet Letter*, and the prefaces in which Henry James expounds the aesthetic principles of his fiction. In the hands of some writers a didactic impulse can virtually turn the supplement into the main text: George Bernard Shaw prefaces his plays with political essays that often seem more substantial than what follows them.

Sometimes the preface is provided by an editor, not by the author; and sometimes the author pretends to be a mere editor. *Moll Flanders* (1722) is known to literary history as a novel written by Daniel Defoe; but neither that genre nor that authorial attribution is indicated on the book's original title page. The narrative is presented there as 'written from her own memorandums'—and the tongue-in-cheek preface states that

> the world is so taken up of late with novels and romances, that
> it will be hard for a private history to be taken as genuine, where
> the names and other circumstances of the person are concealed,
> and on this account we must be content to leave the reader to

pass his own opinion upon the ensuing sheets, and take it just as he pleases.

The pretence may be transparent, but in a puritanical age it served to protect the undeclared real author, Defoe, from any charge of immorality, since the supposed author is Moll, and the preface goes on to claim that an (anonymous) editorialising hand has simply put her story into 'language fit to be read' and deleted anything that might be at odds with 'virtuous and religious uses' of the story.

Editorial or pseudo-editorial instructions about a text's proper 'uses' need not, of course, be taken at face value. Most readers do not hesitate to interpret the preface of *Moll Flanders* as ironical in tone. When John Frow remarks (1986:221) that frames serve to establish metacommunicative conventions, 'specifying how to use the text, what one can expect to happen at different stages, and what to do if these expectations are not confirmed (for example, how to switch frame)', he is allowing for the possibility of reading explicit circumtextual cues in the light of implicit cues. As we noted in an earlier chapter, reliable metamessages are seldom conveyed overtly, and therefore if a metamessage is announced as such it will generally seem to invite reframing as ironic: a kind of meta-metamessage.

Borderline deceptions

It is clear that prefaces may sometimes be unreliable, as in the case of *Moll Flanders*. They may make spurious claims of authority and origin (the 'found manuscript'), and thus permit the supposedly 'informative' editorial circumtext to be contaminated by fiction. The inside/outside distinction, always problematic, is shown in such instances to be entirely unstable. In extreme cases, false circumtexts may be regarded as constructing hoaxes. But in this respect the true/false criterion is generically variable: readers do not apply the same expectations to prose as to lyric poetry, in which the author is normally regarded as almost identical with the speaking subject. This is the convention that James McPherson violated by declaring on the title page of *Fingal: An Ancient Epic Poem* (1762) that he was merely its translator, and that 'Ossian the son of Fingal' composed the Gaelic original—a claim then amplified by an 'Advertisement', a 'Preface' and a 'Dissertation concerning the Antiquity &c. of the Poems of Ossian the Son of Fingal'—whereas in fact McPherson had invented the lot. Defoe's dissimulation about the true authorship of *Moll Flanders* is thought a clever literary technique; McPherson's dissimulation in a different genre led to the charge of imposture.

Hoaxes and forgeries (as distinct from semi-transparent fictions of authorship) are uncommon. But circumtextual features of prose writings may often 'deceive' us in playful ways, for instance through covert puns and slippage of meanings. Marguerite Duras' *L'Amante anglaise* has nothing to do with English lovers; rather, its title alludes to the central character's misspelling of 'English mint' (*la menthe anglaise*), a herb which plays an important thematic role in the text. Alain Robbe-Grillet's novel *La Jalousie* plays on the double meaning of the French word, suggesting both the emotion 'jealousy' and the voyeuristic opportunity offered by the venetian blinds constantly referred to in the novel. Initiated circumtextually, such ambiguities continue to complicate the reader's own role. With particular reference to this novel, MacLachlan (1990) argues that irresolvable tensions between different framing options can pro-duce an unstable interpretive position that may be characterised as a 'jealous mode of reading'. The same Robbe-Grillet text also reminds us that not only title and preface but also cover blurb can mislead: on the cover of an early edition of *La Jalousie* there appeared an authorial statement which seemed to contradict intratextual evidence and which the author himself referred to later in an interview as a 'false key' to the novel's interpretation.

In a book-length prose work, the title conventionally belongs to the 'outer' rim—though there are a few transgressive cases like Italo Calvino's *If On a Winter's Night a Traveller*, where the incomplete and conditional syntax of the title draws attention to its playful link with the 'inner' text, a link that is further indicated by the quasi-acrostic structure of the contents page. But there is always some-thing arbitrary about the notion of a circumtextual border, and defining its extent can be problematic in many instances. Calvino makes this point prominent by beginning the first paragraph of Chapter 1 with a direct address to the reader: 'You are about to begin reading Italo Calvino's new novel'—and beginning the chapter's last paragraph with these words: 'So here you are now, ready to attack the first lines of the first page'. Most of the chapter spins out an amusing preamble to the act of reading which is in fact already under way, and 'this circling of the book, this reading around it before reading inside it' amounts to a demonstration that any line between inside and outside is thoroughly problematic (Calvino, 1982:9, 13). Such tactics are not confined to postmodern fiction. With regard to Hawthorne's *The House of the Seven Gables: A Romance*, published some 140 years before Calvino's novel, it would be reasonable to say that the circumtext includes not only that title and authorial name but also the preface, which begins by glossing the subtitle: 'When a writer calls his work a Romance, it need hardly be observed that he wishes to claim a certain latitude, both as to its fashion and material, which he would not have felt himself entitled to assume had he professed to be writing a Novel'. Yet a reader continues to encounter preliminaries even after moving through the preface. A page into Chapter 1, there is the announcement that we are about to 'commence the real action of our tale'— whereupon many pages are spent recounting events long past, and then the first chapter concludes with a promise that we will now 'proceed to open our narrative'. Such examples make it clear that our term 'circumtext', while a convenient shorthand, is hardly appropriate in so far as it suggests something tangible and fixed.

As we have argued, the line between inside and outside is never free of paradox. This point is not always recognised; the Russian Formalist Jurij Lotman, for instance, insists categorically that 'the frame of a literary work consists of two elements: the beginning and the end' (1977:212, 215), while his compatriot Boris Uspensky declares without qualification that 'the frame is the borderline between the internal world of the representation and the world external to the representation' (1973:143). The difficulty with their matter-of-fact view becomes obvious as soon as one tries to apply it. If, for instance, a brief conventional formula such as 'Once upon a time' or 'The End' seems to constitute part of the circumtext, then where is the line to be drawn with regard to more elaborate prologues and epilogues? Where does the 'outside' of the text meet (or become) its 'inside'? The question cannot be answered in terms of formal features alone. While a literary text always presents itself to us already framed, it must nevertheless undergo our framing of it, just as our framing of it is conversely subject to the framing strategies of the text. Formalist views such as Lotman's and Uspensky's, like Smith's (discussed above in relation to poetry), will tend, as David Carroll observes, 'to ignore the paradoxical status of the frame—even one projected by the literary text itself—and refuse to make the frame work except as a barrier betwen literature and its contexts' (1987:145).

Frames within frames

The more extended and complex a piece of literary prose is, the more important are its various intratextual markers, its frames within frames. As readers we keep wanting to know what stage we have reached in the text, because interpretation is oriented by that knowledge. Written texts, unless they are very brief, require a reader to carry along a great deal of accumulated information and to understand any details in terms of their position in a temporally unfolding sequence. This can be complicated by texts which offer readers the 'freedom' to construct their own reading itinerary. Julio Cortázar's *Hopscotch*, for example, proposes in a 'Table of Instructions' two possible orders of reading the chapters.

How one initially gets one's bearings in a prose narrative depends in part on the particular framing perspective established by the method of narration. Critics still often call this the text's 'point of view', though—as Gérard Genette (1980:185ff.) reminds us—it includes not only the angle from which events are seen but also the angle from which they are narrated: we need to ask who speaks, as well as who sees. This pair of questions cannot always be answered simply, because some texts embed one point of view inside another. In any case, there is no direct correspondence between a particular point of view in a text (as registered in the grammatical person of its narrator) and any particular genre. For instance the foregrounding of subjectivity in first-person narration can be associated either with the conventions of realism (as in most autobiographies, or in the fictional stories purportedly told by Moll Flanders and Robinson Crusoe) or with a display of artifice (as in Tristram Shandy's narrrative).

Broadly categorised, intratextual frames are of two kinds, corresponding to the dual dimensions of the reading process. On the one hand we read as a temporal activity; what has gone before serves as a frame for what follows, and our anticipation of what follows can also affect interpretation, for instance when we notice how little reading time remains as we approach the end of a detective story. On the other hand reading is also a spatial activity, and although prose normally makes less obvious use of that dimension than verse does, nevertheless the subsections and other intratextual devices can frame a novel or a newspaper article or a legal document in distinctive ways. Some prose writings exploit the possibilities of spatial arrangements with great gusto, as Derrida does in the dialogic layout of his essay *Glas* (1974), which incorporates a double column on every page and also disrupts the usual continuity of prose with various quotations and other inserted items. But even the most orthodox writings may signal shifts in frame through the use of italics, paragraph and chapter breaks, roughly corresponding to line and stanza divisions in the case of poetry.

What counts as a line of internal demarcation or as a discrete subsection will depend in part on the eye of the beholder. In her study of *Reading Frames in Modern Fiction* Mary Ann Caws looks at an assortment of extended narrative texts, concentrating on those passages which seem to her to 'stand out in relief from the flow of prose and create, in so standing, different expectations and different effects' (1985:xi). Primarily the kind of framing that interests her is intratextual, though she does not use the term or problematise the concept. Not for her the parergonal paradoxes of Derrida, which she mentions in a passing sentence only in order to dissociate her own line of enquiry from his. 'The question of where the frame is said to be', she comments briskly, '. . . is of less concern to me here than the effect of the actual passages I read as framed within the texts and the recognition of their borders' (ibid.:13). Caws sees few difficulties in the view that, within an ongoing text, 'we perceive borders as if signalled by alterations of pattern and architectural, verbal, or diegetic clues' (ibid.:xi). In an impressionistic rather than theoretically rigorous way, she distinguishes between various framing effects in fiction, such as 'outlining' and 'insetting', and gives detailed readings of their function in a range of novels and stories. Her most useful observation is that 'whereas the passages so marked in "pre-modernist" texts generally call attention to the substance and the field included or stressed, the principal texts of modernism emphasise the very idea of framing as it calls attention, above all, to itself, and to the frames rather than what they include' (ibid.:xi). In particular, the fictions of James, Proust and Woolf are shown to be highly sophisticated in the reflexivity of their framing.

The impressionistic approach taken by Caws is not uniquely hers. In a book on visual structures in Thomas Hardy's novels (which are also discussed at length in Caws's study), Sheila Berger (1990) devotes a chapter to their 'framed images', though without much theoretical precision. There are also several studies of individual prose works in terms of their framing structures and strategies. For instance *Wuthering Heights* is seen as 'preoccupied with the idea of boundary' (Matthews, 1985:26), particularly in its deployment of narratorial frames to enclose the Earnshaw/Linton and Catherine/Heathcliff stories within the interpretive governance of Nelly Dean and Lockwood. But such analyses shed little light on the general question of how interpretive cues and controls operate within the reading process.

Of wider theoretical application are those studies that consider the metacommunicative function of embedded stories and scenes. Lucien Dällenbach (1989) provides a comprehensive account of mirror effects within narratives—the duplicative phenomenon that André Gide called a *mise en abyme*. This covers several varieties of reflexive framing, among which the tale-within-a-tale structure can be particularly resourceful as an inset model of the text that encloses it. In the same vein, Marie Maclean's book on Baudelaire's short narratives looks at his intratextual use of tableau spectacles and performance spaces. Since frames generally serve to demarcate a semiotic field, they can do so not only at the level of the text as a whole but also in miniature, marking off sub-fields within the text. When these embedded effects portray 'not just the actors within the frame but the spectator as voyeur' (Maclean, 1988:12), they may be read as representing aspects of the relation that the text is establishing with its readers. Maclean analyses a number of Baudelaire's prose texts in these terms, with particular reference to changes in the status of the speech acts that are involved. As she notes (ibid.:26), such changes are similar to those described by

Goffman as 'keying'. When an audience is embedded micro-cosmically, the text opens up a space for interpretation because it is drawing attention to the way its intratextual frames comment implicitly on its own status as message (for example, showing that reading is a voyeuristic act). This point is developed in an article by Angela Moger on 'frames of desire' in Maupassant's fiction that are shaped by a special version of the tale-within-a-tale structure. She observes that

> a provocative constant of Maupassant's narrative technique is the rapid introduction, within a slender containing narrative, of a narrator persona responsible for presenting the drama at the heart of the story. The 'primary', or initial, narrator exists only to introduce, on the first page of each story, this 'authorial' figure and, on the last page, that teller's audience. (Moger, 1985:315)

As the embedded story in such cases is obviously the main one, the embedding level of narration may appear superfluous; but Moger shows that the device of an additional narrator and narratee has an important function. Paradoxically it works against closure, situating the reader in a metacommunicative space where the text can 'elucidate rhetorically the properties and potential effects of stories', so as to reveal their subterfuges (ibid.:323–4).

In some multi-story texts, the framing level of narration acquires a particular importance. Its narrator may be presented as a fictional character who nevertheless superintends the telling of tales; thus Scheherazade's own frame tale in *The Arabian Nights* can be interpreted as providing a cohesive theme for the whole collection in its representation of male–female relationships within a particular ideology of dominance (Attar and Fischer, 1991). Or the narrator of a multi-story text may be presented as a quasi-authorial figure of the kind known to structuralist narratology as 'extradiegetic' (Rimmon-Kenan, 1983:91–4), which is the case with Boccaccio's *Decameron*. In a study of this work, Joy Hambuechen Potter concentrates on the function of its *cornice* or frame tale, regarding it as the index to other frames that she finds within the text as a whole. Potter refers to Goffman, Bateson, and other social theorists, but her main assumptions are drawn from Uspensky and Lotman. Some readers will find her analysis of 'the carefully constructed series of frames and frame breaks' in the *Decameron* to be unduly schematic, since it barely acknowledges the paradoxical nature of any subdivision of a text into exterior and interior parts. What she admires is the 'architectonic structure' she finds in Boccaccio's opus: 'The stately and ritualised life of the ten extremely stylised protagonists frames the opening and the closing of each day of storytelling in much the same way as the decorative motifs and pillars or figures that were used to divide or frame the narrative sequences in frescoes or in sculptured works' (Potter, 1982:118). While noting various frame-breaks that are effected through changes of register, she sees these simply in terms of authorial ambivalence—'Boccaccio the escapist' versus 'Boccaccio the realist' (ibid.:122–3).

The more realistic a work of prose fiction aspires to be, the less prominent are its intratextual framing devices. Just as the kind of film that aims at verisimilitude will tend to favour a seamless editing technique, so too any chapter subdivisions in a social realist novel will not draw attention to themselves with the self-conscious labelling found in works of comic artifice. When we encounter in George Meredith's novel *The Egoist* a chapter that is headed 'Sir Willoughby Attempts and Achieves Pathos', or in Voltaire's *Candide* a chapter that is headed 'What Happened to the Two Travellers with Two Girls, Two Monkeys, and the Savages Named Biglugs', we know that we are *not* dealing with the generic conventions of realism. Realist fiction generally tries to make frames and framers invisible. In contrast, intratextual devices are reflexive in function: they highlight the text's own framing, and in their most elaborate forms they can be wily, sportive, duplicitous.

Intertextual framings

Any element of a text can have an intertextual aspect. For instance, while titles themselves serve a circumtextual function, they may need to be framed in relation to other titles in order to be properly understood. As Marie Maclean remarks in discussing 'the art of the peripheral', this kind of intertextual appeal 'works both by inclusion and by exclusion. A readership which identifies the quotation or the style will accept being led by the author toward a specific intertext the more willingly because their vanity is flattered by being "in the know"' (1991:275). Thus Gustave Flaubert, in giving his 1856 novel the name *Madame Bovary*, announces an unromantic story of bourgeois life through the implied contrast with traditional single-name titles of romantic novels such as Prosper Mérimée's *Carmen* or Benjamin Constant's *Adolphe*. Sometimes a title refers specifically to a single prior text, though not in a way that indicates precisely what kind of relation the two texts have. Anyone who sees on a shelf Julian Barnes's book *Flaubert's Parrot* and who knows Flaubert's story 'A Simple Heart' will expect some linkage but needs to begin reading to find out just what it is. Anyone knowing Yeats's poem 'The Second Coming' will recognise a phrase from it in the title of Chinua Achebe's novel *Things Fall Apart*, but again the significance of that allusion becomes clear only as one reads through Achebe's text and encounters there some alternative images for framing the story of its main character Okonkwo (see Reid 1992:70–2). On the other hand, the final line of that same poem by Yeats is reframed with more obvious intent in the title of Peter de Vries's novel *Slouching Towards Kalamazoo*. By substituting the odd name of a midwestern American town, the novelist turns the poet's sinister image of a rough beast that 'slouches towards Bethlehem to be born' into an image of comic bathos, playing on the 'zoo' in Kalamazoo. Thus the tone of the novel is provisionally declared from the outset.

Considered in themselves, however, titles and other circumtextual elements have a relatively limited intertextual scope. Prose texts of any amplitude are likely to embody within the texture of their writing several transformative relationships with other texts or text-types. Even a seemingly simple tale can use framing strategies to achieve intricate generic effects, as Reid (1992:51 ff.) shows in discussing the various affiliations of a story by Alphonse Daudet.

Like any other reference point for interpretation, intertextuality is institutionally framed. That is, our attempts to make sense of anything will depend in part on the particular setting in which we encounter it, and this setting may include for example an educational programme. Just as galleries can exploit or even create the relationship between one art work and another, intertextual relations between texts can be lifted into recognition by being deliberately juxtaposed in a university course. Parts of some English department curricula are now constructed on this principle, with the intention that a student who (for example) reads Charlotte Brontë's *Jane Eyre* and Jean Rhys's *Wide Sargasso Sea* side by side will be observing how one text recasts certain motifs from the other in such a way that nineteenth-century British assumptions about gender, class and nation undergo a postcolonial transvaluation. Though useful as a pedagogic device, this kind of linkage concentrates on a dialectic of priority and subversion. Therefore it may tend to overlook other aspects of intertextuality that are often made prominent in postmodernist texts—such as the way in which fiction increasingly seems to absorb 'fact', or the way in which some contemporary writers engage in a game of rewriting their own texts (as Marguerite Duras does—cf. Reid, 1992:102) or each other's (as Frank Moorhouse and Michael Wilding do—cf. Reid, 1992:ch. 5). These postmodernist moves can radically destabilise the conventional basis of generic reading, seeming to dissolve everything into textuality.

Paratextuality and postmodernist prose

In discussing the generic playfulness of historiographic metafiction, Linda Hutcheon collapses several kinds of framing into the generalised category of 'paratextuality', a term she borrows from Genette. Hutcheon remarks that postmodernist novels such as John Fowles's *A Maggot* or Timothy Findley's *Famous Last Words* incorporate 'the intertexts of history, its documents or its traces' into an avowedly fictional text by using techniques which are often 'those of history-writing, especially its "paratextual" conventions: in particular, its footnotes and illustrations, but also its subtitles, prefaces, epilogues, epigraphs, and so on' (Hutcheon, 1989:82). Commenting further on the work that footnotes perform in a such a novel, she says their function is 'extratextual, referring us to a world outside the novel, but there is something else going on too: most of the notes refer us explicitly to other *texts*' (ibid.:84). In other words they also operate intertextually, and 'this postmodern use of paratextuality as a formal mode of overt intertextuality both works within and subverts that apparatus of realism still typical of the novel genre, even in its more metafictional forms' (ibid.:89). Hutcheon's comments on each device are accurate enough, but to consider all such devices (intertextual, extratextual, intratextual and circumtextual) as forms of a generalised 'paratextuality' is to blur important analytical distinctions.

The problem goes beyond Hutcheon's usage. As expounded initially by Genette, the concept of paratextuality already lacks precision. In part it refers to circumtextual features—to the 'exterior presentation of a book, name of the author, title' and so on. Regarding such features, Genette remarks that, 'rather than with a limit or a sealed frontier, we are dealing in this case with a *threshold*' (Genette, 1991:261–2). In his book *Seuils* (the word means thresholds), he extends paratextuality to cover extremely diverse phenomena. In an ample sense, he argues, 'there does not exist, and there never has existed, a text without a paratext' (ibid.:263). Genette distinguishes broadly between two kinds of paratextual phenomena: the 'peritext', spatially situated in or around the text itself, and the 'epitext', which comprises all those additional external items that can be generated in relation to a text (reviews, interviews with the author, relevant correspondence, and the like). Genette's brand of structuralism leans heavily towards the taxonomic, and much of what he says about paratextuality is taken up with an elaborate inventory of its 'spatial, temporal, substantial, pragmatic, and functional characteristics' (ibid.:263 ff.), each of these further subclassified. Ironically, despite the proliferation of categories, Genette's notion of the peritext remains too general. It does not distinguish pragmatically between those framing items that strike a reader as prefixed or suffixed to the text (for instance information on a book cover), which we call circumtextual, and those items that seem to disrupt internally the reading process (for instance a play within a play, or subsectional titles), which we call intratextual. Genette also tends to fix paratextual features in the reified forms of 'paratext', 'peritext' and 'epitext', as if each of these had a stable and tangible reality. While our own discussion has occasionally used terms such as 'circumtext' for convenience, we have emphasised the provisional and perceptual status of any such factors.

Genette's study of paratextuality is full of intelligent observations about several aspects of framing, and its blend of erudition and humour 'turns a potential catalogue into a constant entertainment', as Maclean (1991:273) remarks appreciatively. But it remains somewhat limited by the fact that its emphasis falls mainly on the liminal—on a reader's point of entry into the text—rather than on the metacommunicative. Certainly he is well aware that framing elements constitute, 'between the text and what lies outside it, a zone not just of transition, but of *transaction*' (Genette, 1991:261); and yet this insight is not fully carried through. He gives relatively little consideration to the power-plays through which texts, in marking their perimeters for us, also inscribe metamessages about the way we interpret the messages they contain. Some political implications of this metacommunicative function of framing will be taken up in our concluding chapter.

6

Markers, Metamessages and Mediation

Texts are always mediated

Discourse analysts, information theorists and literary critics all tell us in their different ways that communication is a mediated activity. This means that messages cannot be beamed directly from sender to receiver. If it were possible to bypass the codes and channels through which meaning is produced, then the discrepancies between what is said, what is meant, and what is understood (discussed at length in Chapter 3) could not occur. The message sent would always be identical with the message received, and this is clearly not the case. As Ross Chambers puts it in an unpublished paper called 'Scandals of Mediation', communication is 'an affair of implicated *understanding*, where understanding implies the unavoidable necessity (from the "receiving" point of view) of "interpretation" and (on the "sending" end) of "readability"'.

In a semiotic perspective, what Chambers calls 'readability' can be thought of as that metacommunicative space where messages about how to interpret the message are encoded. As the present book has emphasised, it is through the framing potentialities offered by any particular message system that a metacommunicative space opens up. In written texts, circumtextual frames associated with the material packaging of the text have the capacity to carry the most obvious messages about how the text should be read. Being liminal or threshold phenomena, as Genette (1987) stresses, they are also likely to be the first messages of this kind that we encounter in the reading process. Other factors, intratextual and intertextual, may reinforce or extend or be at odds with the kinds of messages conveyed by the circumtext.

The importance of these issues across a wide range of contexts has been noted in previous chapters. For example, sociolinguists and speech ethnographers tell us that in face-to-face verbal communication, paralinguistic and prosodic features (as well as features shared with written texts) carry metamessages that affect how we interpret what people say. An inability to encode or decode such messages makes it impossible, according to psychiatrists like Bateson (1972), to negotiate normal relationships with others. Sociologists like Goffman (1974) draw attention to the ways in which frame-setting cues or metamessages are vulnerable to manipulation by others. In Chapter 2 we discussed the metamessages carried by those frames that are specific to visual sign systems such as painting and film, and how they influence our interpretation of what we see and hear. We have also seen that written texts vary in their metacommunicative scope: epitaphs generally offer more limited opportunities for messages of this kind than novels.

If 'readability' (in Chambers' sense) can be thought of as the sum of the metacommunicative messages sent by texts, then 'interpretation' is its corollary, as he states. Readability is the necessary condition for interpretation; conversely, interpretation presupposes that texts have a metacommunicative dimension that makes them 'readable'. And yet, as we have insisted throughout this book, interpretation is not simply a matter of receiving textually encoded messages (or, for that matter, metamessages). Meanings are made or produced by readers and texts in tandem, rather than simply transmitted to one another. (The terms 'text' and 'reader' are used here in their broadest sense.) The meanings we produce are the result of interactions between the text's own framing potentiality (its metamessages) and extratextual framing factors. These determine how we initially constitute or recognise a textual field, and which textual messages within that field we will be most attentive to. The particular extratextual frames applied to a text depend in part, as we noted in Chapter 4, on background knowledge of an experiential or socio-cognitive kind, activated in the reading process. How we interpret a particular text also depends, as we noted, on the broader ideological, socio-cultural and institutional frames that constitute the setting for our reading of it. Being 'an affair of implicated understanding', interpretation is necessarily an interactive process, an ongoing struggle between text and reader for control of the textual field.

Metaphors of framing can therefore draw attention not only to the mediated status of all communication but also to questions of control. Inequalities in power between participants in an exchange will determine who can say what and to whom, who has the right to speak or to remain silent, and who has (or presumes) the right to speak for others. In most communicative situations, our awareness of the mediating power structures that lend authority to certain kinds of discourse tends to be suppressed. But as Chambers reminds us, even messages that we think of as perfectly literal exert authority, and this authority is derived from the contextual relations implied by the message. Teaching French verbs or telling a child to go to bed have more than a literal meaning, backed as they are by institutionalised (familial and educational) relations of power.

Like all frames, however, these authorising structures usually recede into the background. Most of the time, messages tend to be regarded as spontaneous and direct expressions of an individual consciousness. As Michel Serres (1982) remarks, using a metaphor from information theory, the more we are a functioning part of 'the system', the less we perceive the 'noise' in the system. By noise or interference he means anything that impedes the direct transmission of a message, and therefore gives rise to interpretation. Paradoxically, noise is an integral part of the system; indeed it is the element which constitutes the system, because there can be no noise-free, unmediated communication. An observer within the system, says Serres, normally 'overvalues the message and undervalues the noise', repressing the fact of interference 'in order to send or receive communications better and to make them circulate in a distinct and workable fashion' (1982:68). Such repression, Serres suggests, not only involves psychological processes at the individual level but may have broader social and political consequences—religious excommunication, political imprisonment, the isolation of the sick, and so on. Written texts, by foregrounding their mediated status, can draw attention to these issues.

The politics of cultural mediation

It is clear enough in theory, though often forgotten in the reading process, that written texts depend on particularly complex forms of framing. Writer and reader are engaged (albeit unconsciously) in a power struggle through which each tries to control interpretation of the text. But while written texts may complicate the instability in particular ways (see Reid, 1992), we have also noted that no process of communicative exchange is ever reciprocally balanced. The present book argues that different framing factors are always operative in any text or cultural activity, and together they bring power into play. Nevertheless, one thing that makes written texts, and especially literary fictions, so useful to the cultural theorist is that their medium allows them to frame their politics in highly intricate ways.

Some of those intricacies can be registered in the physical construction of a text—its shape, its size, its devices for setting (or questioning) its boundaries. These physical aspects are not simply markers; they convey metamessages as well. Consider a fascinating case in which the cultural politics of a multiple-frame text (or cluster of texts) are demonstrated with unusual explicitness. In East Berlin in 1980 a postmodernist and post-Marxist play called *Der Auftrag* (*The Commission*), written and directed by Heiner Müller, is first performed. It deals with the experiences of revolutionary emissaries from the French Republic who go to the British colony of Jamaica in the 1790s to promote the ideals of liberty, equality and fraternity among the slaves there, following the establishment in nearby Haiti of the Negro Republic of Toussaint L'Ouverture. In 1993, an English version of Müller's play is published in Australia as part of a book which also includes a great deal else. Edited by the German-born Australian academic Gerhard Fischer, *The Mudrooroo/Müller Project: A Theatrical Casebook* has five main sections. In the first there are two essays: one by Fischer on the evolution of his idea of somehow adapting Müller's play so that it would say something about contemporary Australian politics and 'about the dramaturgy of *framing* a theatre text around another one' (Fischer, 1993:10), and another by the Australian Aboriginal writer Mudrooroo on how (at the instigation of Fischer and Aboriginal man-of-the-theatre Brian Syron) he decided to appropriate Müller's play in such a way as 'to construct a frame with penetrations of Aboriginality' (ibid.:22). The book's second section prints Müller's play in Fischer's translation, along with several brief related items such as part of a story by Müller's compatriot Anna Seghers from which the play drew its initial inspiration and several motifs. The third section contains poems and other pieces by Mudrooroo and his playscript *The Aboriginal Protesters Confront the Declaration of the Australian Republic on 26 January 2001 with the Production of* The Commission *by Heiner Müller*. Section four provides workshop notes by Fischer, an interview with Syron, and a retrospect by Mudrooroo on the way he himself has 'framed the text' (ibid.:144). The final section (apart from appendices) is headed 'Politics', and includes several statements by Aboriginal people on political issues such as the relation between the Australian republican movement and independent Aboriginal sovereignty.

This composite product, brought together by Fischer as *The Mudrooroo/Müller Project*, draws attention to the inescapably political implications of reframing prior texts from a different cultural perspective. Inscribed in the material presentation of the book are words and images that suggest the competing claims of the various cultural frames which mediate writing and reading. On the beautifully designed cover, part of a painting by an Aboriginal artist, 'Wrestling with white spirit', is inset within a picture painted by a German artist, 'Twilight of the West'. Other circumtextual elements accumulate, each alluding implicitly to issues of authority, ownership, and the like. The prefatory pages are full of the names of authors, editors, collaborators, actors and associates, and the publication imprint details seem remarkably complicated. Every aspect of the book's circumtext seems charged with cross-cultural tensions. Signs of intertextuality are also multiple and intricate; they include numerous forms of repetition-with-difference, as in the graphics by Paul Klee and Jimmy Pike. These intertextual elements, too, are inseparable from issues of power.

With all its layerings and positionings, such a format announces the difficulty of achieving any intertextual equilibrium. This is always the case, because any writer who engages with another text—and writing always presupposes prior writings—must deal with the power of that text through some counter-strategy. It may take the form of deferential homage—not always to be taken at face value, for it can be a subtle way of establishing some kind of ascendancy over the intertext. Alternatively it may take the form of parodic imitation, critical rewriting from a different socio-cultural or differently gendered perspective, and so on. Whatever the intentions of the writer, however, overt reference to an intertext inevitably raises questions of positioning and power. In the case of *The Mudrooroo/Müller Project* we have a group of texts engaged in reframing, repositioning and playing off one another in a variety of ways. What is mainly at stake in this particular case are the cultural politics of racial minority groups. Mudrooroo's appropriation of Müller's text can be interpreted as representing resistance to the attempt that the German author's play makes to speak on behalf of another racial group.

Intratextual framings are not confined to the enclosure of Müller's text within Mudrooroo's (and of both within Fischer's), but incorporate other play-within-a-play features which have their own political force—notably the scene in *The Commission* in which the French revolutionaries in Jamaica are dressed up by slaves as Robespierre and Danton. So too with the unevenly segmented structure of the book as a whole, interrupted by posters, photographs, drawings and by the divisions between subsections: each ingredient poses in its own way the political question, Who controls the framing?

'Frames are always framed': the issue of authority

Although the stakes may be very different, critical or theoretical writing is another genre that often foregrounds its intertextual connections within a series of competing readings which attempt to dislodge one another. Consider one exemplary instance, a *locus classicus* of post-structuralist criticism. Barbara Johnson's article 'The Frame of Reference: Poe, Lacan, Derrida' examines intricate links in a cluster of texts: a short story by Poe ('The Purloined Letter'), an interpretation of it by Lacan, and an interpretation by Derrida of Lacan's interpretation of Poe. Johnson shows that Derrida's essay repeats the procedures for which he criticises Lacan, particularly in disregarding the literary frame of Poe's text (Johnson,

1981:479–81). The paradox of Derrida's own 'parergonal logic' requires, as Johnson summarises it, that 'the total inclusion of the "frame" is both mandatory and impossible. The "frame" thus becomes not the borderline between the inside and the outside, but precisely what subverts the applicability of the inside/outside polarity to the act of interpretation' (ibid.:481). For instance Poe's story 'The Purloined Letter' frames itself intertextually in intricate ways, so that there is 'an infinitely regressing *reference* to previous writings' (ibid.:483). In other words, says Johnson, 'the frame is always being framed by part of its contents' (ibid.:484–5). Derrida's way of putting the point is this: 'Our purpose is not to prove that "The Purloined Letter" functions within a frame . . . but to prove that the structure of the effects of framing is such that no totalisation of the border is even possible. Frames are always framed' (1975:99).

It would take a disproportionate amount of space to elucidate here the full implications of this complex series of critical upstagings. But two issues are plain. First, interpretive frames cannot be fixed. As David Carroll remarks: 'In Derrida's work, the critical investigation of the question of the specificity and integrity of art or literature leads to the displacement of the frame separating the "inside" of art and literature from the "outside", as well as to the displacement of the theories dependent on such frames' (1987:154). Second, no attempt to master prior texts by an authoritative reading of them can avoid being subject in its turn to the politics of further reframing. Thus this particular series of critical texts continues to be extended. 'The Purloined Letter' and its interpreters have been further interpreted by Norman Holland (1980), Ross Chambers (1984)— and so the emulative process of purloining authority goes on.

Mediated and 'unmediated' communication

Both sets of texts mentioned above, the Mudrooroo/Müller/Fischer playscripts and the Poe/Lacan/Derrida critical interpretations, are paradigms of literary writing: they declare their intertextual connections and draw attention to the various reframing and counterframing moves that these intertexts induce.

In Chapter 3 we quoted a response to a counterframing move in a context far removed from the literary: 'She took my message and reclassified it. She changed the label which indicated what sort of message it was, and that is, I believe, what she does all the time' (Bateson, 1972:199). Bateson's disapproval of such a tactic—wresting control of the frame established by the psychiatrist figure for a particular exchange—is obvious. Indeed, on the basis of this one exchange, he suggests that the woman's habit of constantly reframing other people's messages was responsible for triggering the mental illness of her son. We will not recapitulate here the contradictory messages at work in Bateson's view of the situation, previously discussed. We simply note that his example seems to endorse the politically conservative view that we must accept the frames set by others, especially if they are in a position of some authority. That authority, whether medical, familial, educational or other, generally remains unacknowledged since the relations of power that mediate exchanges are repressed in most types of discourse. In this respect, literary or critical texts seem to stand apart.

And yet, if we do regard literary and critical texts as the kinds in which authority is often demystified in some way, and in which framing processes are candidly foregrounded, there are dangers in this assumption about their 'difference' from other types of discourse. In the unpublished paper cited earlier in this chapter, Chambers argues that awareness of mediation may paradoxically serve an ideological purpose. This is because we fall into the fallacy of constructing the category of information as if it were 'straightforward and natural—a mode of communication that needs no analysis and whose mediations go unexamined'. 'Information' then is accepted as the discursive norm, something which, unlike literature, is supposedly 'not subject to reading . . . not subject to mediated authority but direct, transparently literal and unchallengeable in its assumption of power'.

Tourism and the quest for unmediated experience

If 'unmediated communication' is recognised as an illusion produced by the marking of a manifestly mediated form like literature as exceptional, similar paradoxes can be seen at work in the tourist experience. In *Framing the Sign* (1988), Culler stresses the semiotic function of the tourist 'marker', a term he borrows from Dean MacCannell's fascinating study *The Tourist* (1976). According to MacCannell, a marker is anything that frames something as a tourist 'sight', such as a plaque, a signpost, a brochure, a souvenir. Like other frames, the marker thus constitutes a particular field for special attention as well as guiding the tourist's view of it. At the same time, tourists not only attend to those special markers which frame a touristic field but (unlike the local inhabitants) persist in regarding everything they see as a sign of Frenchness or Englishness, or as typically Italian or Japanese. If for example a tourist sees a dog in Paris with a scarf tied around its neck, this is likely to be interpreted as signifying Frenchness, whereas a Parisian might simply see it as a cute way of dressing up a dog. Culler describes tourists as 'the unsung armies of semiotics' (1988:155) since to be a tourist is to frame everything as a sign of itself, even when it is not specifically marked as such. What constitutes something as a tourist sight is therefore a particular mode of seeing triggered by the experience of 'otherness'.

At the same time, it would seem that what many a tourist most craves is the unframed sight, the pure, unmediated experience. Culler quotes from Walker Percy's account of tourism some remarks on the paradox of this longing to escape from semiotic mediation. 'Why', asks Percy, 'is it almost impossible to gaze directly at the Grand Canyon and see it for what it is?' (Culler, 1988:162). Percy imagines various ways of recovering the thing-in-itself, none of which, of course, proves effective. Even an indirect approach to the canyon through the wilderness, avoiding all the markers that frame the sight, even getting off the beaten track, 'the most beaten track of all', as he concedes, offers no escape from the oppression of semiotic mediation (ibid.:162).

He then imagines the responses of a couple who come across an authentic, unspoiled village on their travels. Instead of being delighted to encounter something fresh and unmarked by the traces of touristic visitation, the pleasure of this couple, he speculates, is diminished by an anxious desire to have their experience certified or authenticated in some way. What they want is some kind of marker which would attest to its authenticity. This is the problem of the unframed sight or site: 'Without these markers', comments Culler, it could not be experienced as authentic—whence the couple's anxiety, anxiety from the absence of markers. The paradox, the dilemma of authenticity, is that to be experienced as authentic it must be marked as authentic, but when it is marked as authentic it is mediated, a sign of itself, and hence lacks the authenticity of what is truly unspoiled, untouched by mediating cultural codes. (ibid.:164)

In our own culture, much of the time, we forget the frames that mediate all our experience. The relief that tourists usually experience when they return home, and conversely the sense of restive unfulfilment that so often accompanies confrontation with famous tourist sights, both stem from the strain of being constantly aware of the semiotically mediated nature of one's everyday experiences. Romantics yearn after the mirage that Hartman (1954) calls 'the unmediated vision'. A desire to escape framing, mixed with a knowledge of the impossibility of satisfying this desire, is part of the post-Romantic condition that most of us now inhabit.

Bibliography

Abelson, Robert P. (1975) 'Concepts for Representing Mundane Reality in Plans', in Bobrow and Collins (eds) *Representation and Understanding*, pp. 273–309

Attar, Samar and Gerhard Fischer (1991) 'Promiscuity, Emancipation, Submission: The Civilising Process and the Establishment of a Female Role Model in the Frame-Story of *1001 Nights*', *Arabic Studies Quarterly*, 13, 3/4, pp. 1–18

Bandler, R. and J. Grindler, (1979) *Frogs into Princes: Neurolinguistic Programming*, Utah: Real People Press

—— (1982) *Reframing: Neurolinguistic Programming*, Utah: Real People Press

Barthes, Roland (1972) *Mythologies*, trans. A. Lavers, London: Jonathan Cape

Bartlett, Frederick C. ([1932]1972) *Remembering: A Study in Experimental and Social Psychology*, Cambridge: Cambridge University Press

Bateson, Gregory (1972) *Steps to an Ecology of Mind*, San Francisco: Chandler Publishing Company

Bauman, Richard and Joel Sherzer (eds) (1974) *Explorations in the Ethnography of Speaking*, London: Cambridge University Press

Bennett, Tony (1988) *Out of Which Past? Critical Reflections on Australian Museum and Heritage Policy*, Cultural Policy Studies Occasional Paper no. 3, Brisbane: ICPS, Griffith University

Berger, Sheila (1990) *Thomas Hardy and Visual Structures: Fram-*

ing, Disruption, Process, New York: New York University Press

Bernstein, Basil ([1971] 1975) 'On the Classification and Framing of Educational Knowledge', in *Class, Codes and Control: Theoretical Studies Towards a Sociology of Language*, New York: Schocken Books, pp. 202–36

Bobrow, Daniel G. and Allan Collins (eds) (1975) *Representation and Understanding: Studies in Cognitive Science*, New York: Academic Press

Bobrow, Daniel G. and Donald A. Norman (1975) 'Some Principles of Memory Schemata', in Bobrow and Collins (eds) *Representation and Understanding*, pp. 131–50

Bordwell, David (1985) *Narration in the Fiction Film*, London: Methuen

—— (1989) *Making Meaning: Inference and Rhetoric in the Interpretation of Cinema*, Cambridge, Mass.: Harvard University Press

Borges, J. L. (1970) *Labyrinths*, trans. Donald A. Yates and James E. Irby, Harmondsworth: Penguin

Britton, James (1983) 'Writing and the Story World', in Barry M. Kroll and Gordon Wells (eds), *Explorations in the Development of Writing*, Chichester: Wiley, pp. 3–30

Brown, Gillian and George Yule (1983) *Discourse Analysis*, Cambridge: Cambridge University Press

Bruce, Bertram and Denis Newman (1978) 'Interacting Plans', *Cognitive Science*, 2, pp. 195–233

Calvino, Italo (1982) *If On A Winter's Night A Traveller*, trans. William Weaver, London: Picador

Carroll, David (1987) *Paraesthetics: Foucault, Lyotard, Derrida*, New York: Methuen

Carter, Michael (1990) *Framing Art: Introducing Theory and the Visual Image*, Sydney: Hale & Iremonger

Caws, Mary Ann (1985) *Reading Frames in Modern Fiction*, Princeton N.J.: Princeton University Press

Celant, Germano (1982) 'Framed: Innocence or Gilt?', *Artforum*, 20, pp. 49–55

Chafe, W. (1977a) 'Creativity in verbalization and its implications for the nature of stored knowledge', in R. O. Freedle (ed.),

Discourse Production and Comprehension, Norwood, N.J.: Ablex, pp. 41–55

—— (1977b) 'The recall and verbalization of past experience', in R.W. Cole (ed.), *Current issues in linguistic theory*, Bloomington, Indiana: Indiana University Press, pp. 215–46

Chambers, Ross (1979) *Meaning and Meaningfulness: Studies in the Analysis and Interpretation of Texts*, Lexington, Kentucky: French Forum

—— (1984) *Story and Situation. Narrative Seduction and the Power of Fiction*, Minneapolis: University of Minneapolis Press

—— (1986) 'An Address in the Country: Mallarmé and the Kinds of Literary Context', *French Forum*, 11, 2, pp. 199–215

—— (unpub.) 'Scandals of Mediation', paper presented to 1989 conference of the Australasian Universities Language and Literature Association, Sydney

Charniak, E. (1979) 'Ms Malaprop, a language comprehension program', in Metzing (ed.), *Frame Conceptions and Text Understanding*, pp. 62–78

Cole, R. W. (ed.) (1977) *Current issues in linguistic theory*, Bloomington, Indiana: Indiana University Press

Coulthard, Malcolm (1985) *An Introduction to Discourse Analysis*, London & New York: Longman

Culler, Jonathan (1975) *Structuralist Poetics: Structuralism, Linguistics and the Study of Literature*, London: Routledge & Kegan Paul

—— (1988) *Framing the Sign: Criticism and its Institutions*, Oxford: Blackwell

Dällenbach, Lucien (1989) *The Mirror in the Text*, trans. Jeremy Whiteley and Emma Hughes, Cambridge: Polity Press

de Beaugrande, Robert (1980) *Text, Discourse, and Process: Toward a Multidisciplinary Science of Texts*, London: Longman

Deleuze, Gilles and Félix Guattari (1977) *Anti-Œdipus: Capitalism and Schizophrenia*, trans. R. Hurley, M. Seem and H. R. Lane, New York: Viking Press

Derrida, Jacques (1975) 'The Purveyor of Truth', trans. Willis Domingo et al., *Yale French Studies*, 52, pp. 31–113

—— (1976) *Of Grammatology*, trans. Gayatri Chakravorty Spivak, Baltimore: Johns Hopkins University Press

—— (1978) *La Vérité en peinture*, Paris: Flammarion

—— (1982) *Margins of Philosophy*, trans. Alan Bass, London: Harvester Press

—— (1987) *The Truth in Painting*, trans. Geoff Bennington and Ian McLeod, Chicago and London: University of Chicago Press

Douglas, Mary ([1966] 1978) *Purity and Danger*, London: Routledge & Kegan Paul

Eco, Umberto (1979) *The Role of the Reader*, Bloomington: Indiana University Press

—— (1984) *Semiotics and the Philosophy of Language*, London: Macmillan

Eisenstein, Sergei (1949) *Film Form*, trans. Jay Leyda, New York: Harcourt, Brace & World

Eliot, T. S. (1953) *Selected Prose*, ed. John Hayward, Harmondsworth: Penguin

Fairclough, Norman (1989) *Language and Power*, London: Longman

—— (1992) *Discourse and Social Change*, Cambridge: Polity Press

Fillmore, Charles J. (1975) 'An alternative to checklist theories of meaning', in *Proceedings of the First Annual Meeting of the Berkeley Linguistics Society*, University of California, pp. 123–31

—— (1976) 'The need for a frame semantics within linguistics', in *Statistical Methods in Linguistics*, Stockholm: Scriptor, pp. 5–29

—— (1977) 'Scenes and Frame Semantics', in Antonio Zampolli (ed.), *Linguistic Structures Processing*, Amsterdam: North-Holland Publishing Company, pp. 52–82

Fischer, Gerhard (ed.) (1993) *The Mudrooroo/Müller Project: A Theatrical Casebook*, Sydney: New South Wales University Press

Fish, Stanley (1980) *Is There a Text in this Class? The Authority of Interpretive Communities*, Cambridge, Mass.: Harvard University Press

Frake, Charles (1980) 'Plying frames can be dangerous: Some reflections on methodology in cognitive anthropology', in Anwar S. Dil (ed.), *Language and Cultural Description. Essays by Charles O. Frake*, Stanford, California: Stanford University Press, pp. 45–60

Freadman, Anne (1987) 'Anyone for tennis?', in Ian Reid (ed.), *The Place of Genre in Learning: Current Debates*, Geelong: CSLE, Deakin University, pp. 91–124

Free, Renée (1975) *Victorian Olympians*, Sydney: Art Gallery of New South Wales

Freedle, R. O. (ed.) (1977) *Discourse Production and Comprehension*, Norwood, N.J.: Ablex

Freund, Elizabeth (1987) *The Return of the Reader: Reader-Response Criticism*, London and New York: Methuen

Frow, John (1986) *Marxism and Literary History*, Oxford: Blackwell

Gadamer, Hans Georg (1975) *Truth and Method*, New York: Seabury Press

Genette, Gérard (1980) *Narrative Discourse*, trans. Jane E. Lewin, London: Blackwell

—— (1987) *Seuils*, Paris: Seuils

—— (1991) 'Introduction to the Paratext', trans. Marie Maclean, *New Literary History*, 22, pp. 261–72

Gensler, O. (1977) 'Non-syntactic Antecedents and Frame Semantics', *Proceedings of the Third Annual Meeting of the Berkeley Linguistics Society*, University of California, pp. 321–34

Goffman, Erving (1974) *Frame Analysis: An Essay on the Organization of Experience*, Cambridge, Mass: Harvard University Press

—— (1981) *Forms of Talk*, Philadelphia: University of Pennsylvania Press

Goodwin, Marjorie Harness (1990) *He-Said-She-Said: Talk as Social Organisation among Black Children*, Bloomington: Indiana University Press

Gumperz, John J. (1977) 'Sociocultural knowledge in conversational inference', in M. Saville-Troike (ed.) *28th Annual Roundtable*, Monograph series on languages and linguistics, Georgetown: Georgetown University Press

—— (1982a) *Language and Social Identity*, Cambridge: Cambridge University Press

—— (1982b) *Discourse Strategies,* Cambridge: Cambridge University Press

Halliday, M. A. K. and Ruqaiya Hasan (1985) *Language, Context, and Text: Aspects of Language in a Social-Semiotic Perspective*, Geelong: Deakin University Press

Hartman, Geoffrey (1954) *The Unmediated Vision: An Interpreta-*

tion of Wordsworth, Hopkins, Rilke and Valéry, New Haven: Yale University Press

Hastert, Marie Paule and Jean Jacques Weber (1992) 'Power and Mutuality in *Middlemarch*', in Toolan (ed.), *Language, Text and Context: Essays in Stylistics*, pp. 163–81

Hayes, P. J. (1980) 'The Logic of Frames', in Metzing (ed.), *Frame Conceptions and Text Understanding*, pp. 46–61

Heath, Stephen (1981) *Questions of Cinema*, London: Macmillan

Heydenryk, Henry (1963) *The Art History of Frames: An Enquiry into the Enhancement of Paintings*, New York: Heineman

Hirsch, E. D. (1967) *Validity in Interpretation*, New Haven: Yale University Press

Hodge, Bob and Vijay Mishra (1991) *Dark Side of the Dream: Australian Literature and the Postcolonial Mind*, Sydney: Allen & Unwin

—— (1992) 'Semiotics and History', *Meanjin*, 51, 4, pp. 877–83

Holland, Norman (1980) 'Re-Covering "The Purloined Letter": Reading as a Personal Transaction', in Susan R. Suleiman and Inge Crosman (eds), *The Reader in the Text: Essays on Audience and Interpretation*, Princeton: Princeton University Press, pp. 350-70

Hutcheon, Linda (1989) *The Politics of Postmodernism*, London and New York: Routledge

Hymes, Dell (1974) 'Ways of Speaking', in Richard Bauman and Joel Sherzer (eds), *Explorations in the Ethnography of Speaking*, London: Cambridge University Press

Johnson, Barbara (1981) 'The Frame of Reference: Poe, Lacan, Derrida', in *The Critical Difference: Essays in the Contemporary Rhetoric of Reading*, Baltimore: Johns Hopkins University Press, pp. 110-46

Kelly-Byrne, Diana (1991) *The Gendered Framing of English Teaching: A Selective Case Study*, Geelong: CSLE, Deakin University

Kintsch, Walter (1974) *The Representation of Meaning in Memory*, Hillsdale, New Jersey: Lawrence Erlbaum Associates

Kress, Gunther and T. van Leeuwen (1990) *Reading Images*, Geelong: Deakin University Press

Kristeva, Julia (1986) *The Kristeva Reader*, ed. Toril Moi, Oxford: Blackwell

Kuipers, Benjamin, J. (1975) 'A Frame for Frames: Representing

Knowledge for Recognition', in Bobrow and Collins (eds), *Representation and Understanding*, pp. 151–84

Labov, W. and D. Fanshel (1977) *Therapeutic Discourse: Psychotherapy as Conversation*, New York: Academic Press

Lakoff, G. and M. Johnson (1980) *Metaphors We Live By*, Chicago: University of Chicago Press

Lehnert, W. G. (1980) 'The Role of Scripts in Understanding', in Metzing (ed.), *Frame Conceptions and Text Understanding*, pp. 79–95

Levinson, S. (1983) *Pragmatics*, Cambridge: Cambridge University Press

Lotman, Jurij (1977) *The Structure of the Artistic Text*, trans. Gail Lenhoff and Ronald Vroon, Ann Arbor: Michigan Slavic Contributions

MacCannell, Dean (1976) *The Tourist*, New York: Schocken

—— (1992) *Empty Meeting Grounds: The Tourist Papers*, London and New York: Routledge

MacLachlan, Gale (1988) 'The (Set) Text as Genre', *Typereader*, 1, pp. 13–18

—— (1990) 'Reading in the Jealous Mode', *Australian Journal of French Studies*, 27, 3, pp. 291–302

—— (1993) 'The Seductions of Detective Fiction: The Case of San Antonio', *Aumla*, 79, pp. 29–43

Maclean, Marie (1988) *Narrative as Performance: The Baudelairean Experiment*, London: Routledge.

—— (1991) 'Pretexts and Paratexts: The Art of the Peripheral', *New Literary History*, 22, pp. 273–79.

Matthews, John T. (1985) 'Framing in *Wuthering Heights*', *Texas Studies in Literature and Language*, 27, pp. 26–61

Metzing, Dieter (ed.) (1980) *Frame Conceptions and Text Understanding*, Berlin: de Gruyter

Minsky, Marvin (1975) 'A Framework for Representing Knowledge', in P. H. Winston (ed.), *The Psychology of Computer Vision*, New York: McGraw-Hill, pp. 211–77

—— (1980) 'A Framework for Representing Knowledge' [condensed version of 1975 article], in Metzing (ed.), *Frame Conceptions and Text Understanding*, pp. 1–25

—— (1986) *The Society of Mind*, New York: Simon & Schuster

Moger, Angela S. (1985) 'Narrative Structure in Maupassant: Frames of Desire', *PMLA*, 100, 3, pp. 315–27

Monaco, James (1977) *How to Read a Film*, New York: Oxford University Press

Owen, W. J. B. and Jane Worthington Smyser (eds) (1974) *The Prose Works of William Wordsworth*, vol. 2, Oxford: Clarendon Press

Palmer, Richard E. (1969) *Hermeneutics: Interpretation Theory in Schleiermacher, Dilthey, Heidegger, and Gadamer*, Evanston Ill.: Northwestern University Press

Pearson, John H. (1990) 'The Politics of Framing in the Late Nineteenth Century', *Mosaic*, 23, 1, pp. 15–30

Potter, Joy Hambuechen (1982) *Five Frames for the Decameron: Communication and Social Systems in the Cornice*, Princeton: Princeton University Press

Reid, Ian (ed.) (1987) *The Place of Genre in Learning: Current Debates*, Geelong: CSLE, Deakin University

—— (1988a) 'Genre and Framing: the Case of Epitaphs', *Poetics*, 17, pp. 25–35

—— (1988b), 'A Register of Deaths?', in T. L. Burton and Jill Burton (eds) *Lexicographical and Linguistic Studies: Essays in Honour of G. W. Turner*, Cambridge: D. S. Brewer, pp. 103–14

—— (1989), 'When is an Epitaph not an Epitaph? A Monumental Generic Problem and a Jonsonian Instance', *Southern Review*, 22, 3, pp. 198–210

—— (1990) 'Reading as Framing, Writing as Reframing', in Michael Hayhoe and Stephen Parker (eds), *Reading and Response*, Milton Keynes: Open University Press, pp. 49–61

—— (1992) *Narrative Exchanges*, London: Routledge

Ricoeur, Paul (1974) *Hermeneutics and the Human Sciences: Essays on Language, Action and Interpretation*, trans. John B. Thompson, Cambridge: Cambridge University Press

Rimmon-Kenan, Shlomith (1983) *Narrative Fiction: Contemporary Poetics*, London: Methuen.

Rose, Andrea (1992) *The Pre-Raphaelites*, London: Phaidon Press

Rosenberg, S. T. (1980) 'Frame-based Text Processing', in Metzing (ed.), *Frame Conceptions and Text Understanding*, pp. 96–119

Rumelhart, D. E. (1975) 'Notes on a Schema for Stories', in Bobrow

& Collins (eds), *Representation and Understanding*, pp. 211–36

Said, Edward W. (1975) *Beginnings: Intention and Method*, New York: Basic Books

Sándor, András (1990) 'Text, Frame, Discourse', *Semiotica*, 78, 1/2, pp. 51–73

Schank, Roger C. (1975) 'The Structure of Episodes in Memory', in Bobrow and Collins (eds), *Representation and Understanding*, pp. 237–72

Schank, Roger C. and Robert P. Abelson (1977) *Scripts, Plans, Goals and Understanding*, New York: Lawrence Erlbaum Associates

Schapiro, Meyer (1969) 'On Some Problems in the Semiotics of Visual Art', *Semiotica*, 1, 3, pp. 223–42

Serres, Michel (1982) *The Parasite*, trans. Lawrence R. Schehr, Baltimore, Johns Hopkins University Press

Sinclair J. and R. M. Coulthard (1975) *Towards an Analysis of Discourse: the English used by Teachers and Pupils*, Oxford: Oxford University Press

Smith, Barbara Herrnstein (1968) *Poetic Closure: A Study of How Poems End*, Chicago and London: University of Chicago Press

Steiner, Wendy (1982) *The Colors of Rhetoric: Problems in the Relation between Modern Literature and Painting*, Chicago and London: University of Chicago Press

Stern, Lesley (1981) 'Fiction/Film/Femininity', *Australian Journal of Screen Theory*, 9/10, pp. 37–68

Tannen, Deborah (1979) 'What's in a frame? Surface evidence for underlying expectations', in Roy O. Freedle (ed.), *New Directions in Discourse Processing*, Norwood, N.J: Ablex, pp. 137–81

—— (1984) *Conversational Style: Analyzing Talk among Friends*, Norwood, N.J. and London: Ablex

—— (1991) *You Just Don't Understand: Men and Women in Conversation*, London: Virago

—— (1992) *That's Not What I Meant!* London: Virago

Toolan, Michael (ed.) (1992) *Language, Text and Context: Essays in Stylistics*, London and New York: Routledge

Uspensky, Boris (1973) *A Poetics of Composition*, trans. Valentina Zavarin and Susan Wittig, Berkeley: University of California Press van Dijk, Teun A. (1977) *Text and Context*, London: Longman

Verdaasdonk, H. (1982) 'Conceptions of Literature as Frames?', *Poetics*, 11, pp. 87–104.

Wilden, Anthony (1984) 'Montage: Analytic and Dialectic', *American Journal of Semiotics*, 3, 1, pp. 25-47

Wilks, Y. (1980) 'Frames, semantics and novelty', in Metzing (ed.), *Frame Conceptions and Text Understanding*, pp. 134–63

Winograd, Terry (1975) 'Frame representations and the declarative/procedural controversy', in Bobrow and Collins (eds), *Representation and Understanding: Studies in Cognitive Science*, pp. 185–210

Wolfe, Patrick (1992) 'Patrick Wolfe Replies', *Meanjin*, 51, 4, pp. 884–8

Zampolli, Antonio (ed.) (1977) *Linguistic Structures Processing*, Amsterdam: North-Holland Publishing Company

Index

Abelson, Robert, 2, 4, 6, 67–70 *passim*, 75
Achebe, Chinua, 102
Adolphe, 102
Allegory: after Courbet, 30
Andrews, Julie, 37
Angelus, The, 30
Arabian Nights, The, 100
Arrival of the Maoris in New Zealand, The, 24
art, *see* film; literature; painting; sculpture; television; theatre
Attar, Samar, 100

Bandler, R., 46
Barnes, Julian, 102
Barthes, Roland, 15, 92
Bartlett, Frederick, 2, 41, 65–6, 69–70
Bateson, Gregory, 12–13, 41–8, 57, 60–1, 100, 107, 113
Beckett, Samuel, 52
Benjamin, Walter, 35
Berger, Sheila, 99
Bernstein, Basil, 77–81
Beyond a Reasonable Doubt, 38
Boccaccio, Giovanni, 100–1
Boer War, The, 33
border, *see* frame: borders and margins of
Bordwell, David, 12, 34, 35, 38, 39
Borges, J. L., 6
Brack, John, 28

Breathless, 36; *see also* Godard, Jean-Luc
Brontë, Charlotte, 103
Brown, Gillian, 2, 69

Calvino, Italo, 95
Candide, 101
Carmen, 102
Carroll, David, 97, 112
Carter, Michael, 23, 33–4
Caws, Mary Ann, 98–9
Celant, Germano, 24
Cervantes, Miguel de, 93
Cézanne, Paul, 29
Chagall, Marc, 29
Chambers, Ross, 8, 106–8, 112–13
circumtextuality, *see* framing, circumtextual
class, 8, 49, 60, 78, 103
code, 10–11, 35–6, 80–1, 93
cognition, *see* frame: cognitive; framing: and cognition
Collins, Charles, 27
Commission, The, 109
Constant, Benjamin, 102
context, 5–11, 17, 25, 36, 42, 44–5, 58, 61, 65, 68, 70–5 *passim,* 97, 108, 112
Convent Thoughts, 27
Cook, the Thief, the Wife, the Lover, The, 37
Cortázar, Julio, 97

Coulthard, Malcolm, 83
Couple with Heads full of Clouds, 30
Courbet, Gustave, 26, 30
Culler, Jonathan, 7, 9–10, 90, 113–14

Dali, Salvador, 30
Dällenbach, Lucien, 99
Danton, Georges, 111
Daudet, Alphonse, 102
David, Louis, 30
Day for Night, 36; *see also* Truffaut, François
de Andrea, John, 30
de Beaugrande, Robert, 68
de Cervantes, Miguel, *see* Cervantes, Miguel de
de Vries, Peter, 102
Decameron, The, 100–1
Defoe, Daniel, 93, 95
Degas, Edgar, 26
Der Auftrag, see Commission, The
Derain, André, 29
Derrida, Jacques, 6–9, 16, 25, 27, 98, 111–12
Diderot, Denis, 33
Dilthey, Wilhelm, 12
discourse, 4, 10, 14, 26–7, 69–70, 83, 92, 106, 108, 113
Don Quixote, 93
Double Self Portrait, 28
Douglas, Mary, 77
Duchamp, Marcel, 30–1, 91
Duchet, Claude, 93
Duras, Marguerite, 37, 92, 95, 103
Dürer, Albrecht, 28

education, *see* framing: and educational knowledge
Egoist, The, 101
Eisenstein, Sergei, 36
Eliot, T. S., 6
Entombment, The, 29
'Epitaph on Elizabeth, L. H.', 89
Ernst, Max, 29
Escher, M. C., 29
ethnicity, 60
extratextuality, *see* framing: extratextual

Fairclough, Norman, 8–9, 13–14, 68, 70

Famous Last Words, 103
Fillmore, Charles, 73, 74
film, *see* frame: cinematic; framing: and film; *individual directors and titles*
Findley, Timothy, 103
Fingal: An Ancient Epic Poem, 94
Fischer, Gerhard, 100, 109–12 *passim*
Fish, Stanley, 91
Flaubert, Gustave, 102
Flaubert's Parrot, 102
Four Hundred Blows, 36; *see also* Truffaut, François
Fowles, John, 103
Frake, Charles, 71
frame, 2, 6, 17, 25, 39, 47, 49, 54–9, 65, 69, 73, 75; absent, 24; as site of interpretive struggle, 8–9, 11, 18, 23–5, 27–8, 34, 43–4, 56, 59, 63, 79, 83, 93, 108, 111, 113; as 'supplement', 16, 26–7; borders and margins of, 12–13, 15–16, 20, 22–3, 25–6, 28, 51–2, 54–5, 78–9, 83, 94–6; breaking of, 13–15, 28–9, 52; cinematic, 35–7; cognitive, 2, 16–17, 34, 40–1, 75; disputes, 56–7; extra-compositional, 22, 93; functions of, 9, 16, 18, 20, 22–3, 27, 30, 32, 36, 51, 54, 83, 100, 105; gallery/museum as, 9, 13, 31–2; generic, 2, 17; intra-compositional, 24; invisibility of, 6, 19, 21, 25, 34, 55, 64; psychological, 41, 45–6; semantics and, 73–4; soundtrack as, 37; theatrical, 21, 50, 55, 59; traps, 14, 53, 57
framework, 11, 17, 46–8, 56, 58–60, 72, 76; primary, 48–50
framing, 16–17, 45–7, 53, 57, 59, 61, 64–5, 75, 79, 83–5, 115; act of, 4–6, 8, 15, 26, 58, 75, 83; and art, 5, 9, 13, 18–19; and cognition, 70–5; and educational knowledge, 77–80; and film, 34–5, 38, 52, 72; and genre, 91–4, 101; and narrative, 1, 2, 35–6, 52, 66, 83, 91, 97–101; and photography, 5, 39; circumtextual, 4, 31–4, 38, 59, 76, 84, 87, 89, 92, 94–6, 101–2, 104, 106, 110; extratextual, 3–4, 8, 34, 58, 65, 69,

71, 81, 88, 107; intertextual, 4, 8, 29–30, 33, 38, 76, 87–9, 101–2, 107; intratextual, 4, 27, 38, 76, 88–9, 97–101, 104, 107, 111; metacommunicative, 41–5, 58, 61–2, 64, 94, 99, 105, 106; politics of, 11, 60, 108–13; *see also* interpretation
Freadman, Anne, 92
Free, Renée, 25
Freund, Elizabeth, 7
From the Yarra across Melbourne Botanic Gardens, 20
Frow, John, 13, 16, 54, 55, 94

Gadamer, Hans-Georg, 12
gender, 8, 60, 63, 75, 82, 103
Genette, Gérard, 93, 97, 104–6
genre, 4, 14–16, 21, 29, 69–71, 80, 85–105 *passim*; critical theory, 4, 111; detective fiction, 2, 15, 17, 36, 98; epitaph, 86–9; poetry, 90–1, 94–5; prose, 92–105; *see also* frame: generic
Géricault, Théodore, 24, 29
Gide, André, 99
Girlhood of Mary Virgin, The, 27
Godard, Jean-Luc, 36, 37, 52
Goffman, Erving, 14–15, 29, 46–60, 63, 77, 91, 100, 107
Goldie, C. F., 24
Greenaway, Peter, 37
Grindler, J., 46
Gumperz, John, 41, 60, 62

Haley, Alex, 58
Halliday, M. A. K., 86
Hardy, Thomas, 99
Hartman, Geoffrey, 115
Hasan, Ruqaiya, 86
Hawthorne, Nathaniel, 93, 96
Heath, Stephen, 35, 37
Hegel's Holiday, 33, *see also* Magritte, René
Henson, Bill, 32
hermeneutics, 12
Heydenryk, Henry, 20
Hirsch, E. D., 12
Hodge, Bob, 81, 82
Holland, Norman, 112
Horner, Arthur, 6

House of the Seven Gables, The, 96, *see also* Hawthorne, Nathaniel
Hutcheon, Linda, 103–4
Hymnen, 55

If On a Winter's Night a Traveller, 95
India Song, 37–8; *see also* Duras, Marguerite
interpretation, 1–12, 17–18, 27, 32, 34–5, 38, 40–1, 44, 48, 57, 59–60, 65, 70, 75–6, 84–8 *passim,* 91, 97–8, 100, 102, 106–9, 111; *see also* framing
interpreter, 9, 12, 15, 27, 35, 48, 58, 70–4 *passim,* 88, 99, 107; *see also* reader; viewer
intertextuality, *see* framing: intertextual
intratextuality, *see* framing: intratextual

James, Henry, 93, 99
Jane Eyre, 103
Johnson, Barbara, 111
Johnson, Samuel, 86
Jonson, Ben, 89

Kant, Immanuel, 16
Keats, John, 91
Kelly-Byrne, Diana, 82–3
keying, 48–50, 54, 56–7, 100; *see also* rekeying
Klee, Paul, 110
Kristeva, Julia, 88
Kurosawa, Akira, 57

La Chinoise, 52; *see also* Godard, Jean-Luc
La Jalousie, 95
Lacan, Jacques, 111, 112
Lacemaker, The, 30
Lakoff, G., 60
L'Amante anglaise, 95; *see also* Duras, Marguerite
Last Year at Marienbad, 36
Léger, Fernand, 30
Lelouche, Claude, 35
literature, *see individual authors and titles*

Lorrain, Claude, 31
Lotman, Jurij, 96–7, 100

MacCannell, Dean, 114
MacLachlan, Gale, 15, 83, 93, 95
Maclean, Marie, 99, 101, 105
McPherson, James, 94
Madame Bovary, 102
Madame Récamier, 30; *see also* Magritte, René
Maggot, A., 103
Magritte, René, 29, 30, 33
Man and a Woman, A, 35
Manet, Edouard, 28
Maratti, Carlo, 22
margin, *see* frame: borders and margins of
Matthews, John, 99
Melancholia, 28
Melancholy, 28
Meredith, George, 101
Mérimée, Prosper, 102
metamessage, 22, 39, 41–3, 45, 61–5, 77, 93–4, 105–7, 109
Metzing, Dieter, 71, 75
Millais, John Everett, 26
Millet, Jean-François, 30
Milton, John, 92
Minsky, Marvin, 2, 70–5 *passim*, 77
misframing, 14, 56
Mishra, Vijay, 81, 82
modernism, 24, 26, 29, 99
modernity, *see* modernism
Moger, Angela, 100
Moll Flanders, 93
Mona Lisa, 30
Monaco, James, 35, 36
Moore, Dudley, 37
Moorhouse, Frank, 103
Morris, William, 26
Mudrooroo, 109–12 *passim*
Müller, Heiner, 109–12 *passim*
Munch, Edvard, 28

Number twenty-eight, 33

Olympia, 28
Owen, W. J. B., 86

Painter's Studio, The, 30

painting, *see individual artists and titles*
Palmer, Richard, 12
paratextuality, 103–4
parergon, 16, 25, 98, 112
parody, 15–16
Passion, 37; *see also* Godard, Jean-Luc
Pearson, John, 22–7 *passim*, 93
Percy, Walker, 114
Petyarre, Mavis Holmes, 22
Picasso, Pablo, 21
Pike, Jimmy, 110
Pirandello, Luigi, 52
Poe, Edgar Allan, 112
Pollock, Jackson, 33
Potter, Joy Hambuechen, 100
Poynter, Sir Edward, 24
Proust, Marcel, 99
'Purloined Letter, The', 112

race, 8, 60, 109, 111
Raft of the Medusa, 24
Rashomon, 57–8
reader, 2–3, 11, 15, 36, 52, 70, 85–8, 90, 92–3, 95, 97, 100, 104, 107–9; *see also* interpreter; viewer
reading, *see* interpretation
Rear Window, 38
Red Carpet, 28
reframing, 6, 18, 31, 36, 46–7, 63, 76, 112–13
Reid, Ian, 83, 86, 88–9, 102–3, 109
rekeying, 50; *see also* keying
Renoir, Auguste, 26
Resnais, Alain, 36
Rhys, Jean, 103
Ricoeur, Paul, 12
Rimbaud, Arthur, 5, 6, 8
Rimmon-Kenan, Shlomith, 100
Robbe-Grillet, Alain, 95
Robespierre, Maximilien de, 111
Roots, 58
Rose, Andrea, 33
Rossetti, Christina, 33
Rossetti, Dante Gabriel, 27
Rumelhart, D. E., 70

San-Antonio, 15 ·
Scarlet Letter, The, 93; *see also*

Hawthorne, Nathaniel
Schank, Roger, 2, 4, 6, 67–70, 75
Schapiro, Meyer, 19–29 *passim*
schemata, 2, 41, 65, 70, 72
Schleiermacher, Friedrich, 12
script, 2–4, 70, 72, 75–6
sculpture, *see* de Andrea, John
'Second Coming, The', 102
Seghers, Anna, 110
semantics, *see* frame: and semantics
semiotics, 10–12 *passim*, 23, 45, 82,
   114
Serres, Michel, 108
Seurat, Georges, 26
Seven Deadly Sins, 50
sex, lies and videotape, 38
sexuality, 60
Shakespeare, William, 56
Shaw, George Bernard, 93
Shaw, John Byam, 33
Shoot the Pianist, 37; *see also* Truffaut,
   François
Sidney, Sir Philip, 92
'Simple Heart, A', 102
Sinclair, J., 83
Slouching Towards Kalamazoo, 102
Smith, Barbara Herrnstein, 90–2, 97
Smyser, Jane Worthington, 86
*Son nom de Vénise dans Calcutta
   désert,* 37; *see also* Duras, Margue-
   rite
Sontag, Susan, 52
spectator, 28, 35, 99; *see also* viewer
Steele, L. J., 24
Stockhausen, Karlheinz, 55
Streeton, Arthur, 20
Syron, Brian, 109

Tannen, Deborah, 2, 40–1, 60–70, 89
Taylor, Howard, 28
television, *see Seven Deadly Sins*

10 (film), 37
text, 10, 17, 54, 66, 70–1, 83–4, 100,
   107, 109; production, 7–10, 17, 31,
   71; reception, 7–9, 32, 67, 71, 81,
   86
theatre, *see Commission, The; Hymnen*
Things Fall Apart, 102
This is not a pipe, 33; *see also* Magritte,
   René
This is not a short story, 33
Titian (Tiziano Vecellio), 29
Toulouse-Lautrec, Henri de, 26
Truffaut, François, 36, 37
Turner, J. M. W., 29, 31

Uspensky, Boris, 39, 52, 96–7, 100

Verdaasdonk, H., 89
Vermeer, Jan, 30
viewer, 6, 11, 20, 22–5, 27–30 *passim*,
   33, 35–8 *passim*, 52, 69; *see also*
   interpreter; spectator
*Visit of the Queen of Sheba to King
   Solomon, The,* 24
Voltaire, 101

Walwicz, Ania, 84
War of the Worlds, The, 59
Warhol, Andy, 31
Welles, Orson, 59
Wells, H. G., 59
Whiteley, Brett, 5–9 *passim*
Wide Sargasso Sea, 103
Wilding, Michael, 103
Wolfe, Patrick, 82
Woolf, Virginia, 99
Wuthering Heights, 99
Wyatt, Thomas, 91

Yeats, W. B., 102
Yule, George, 2, 69